D1553477

Children and Play in the Holocaust

Children and Play in the Holocaust

Games among the Shadows

George Eisen

The University of Massachusetts Press
Amherst, 1988

Printed in the United States of America
Designed by Edith Kearney
Set in Linoterm Palatino
Printed by Thomson-Shore, Inc.
and bound by John H. Dekker & Sons, Inc.

Library of Congress Cataloging-in-Publication Data
Eisen, George, 1943–
Children and play in the Holocaust: games among the shadows / George Eisen.
p. cm.
Bibliography: p.
Includes index.
ISBN 0–87023–621–0 (alk. paper)
1. Holocaust, Jewish (1939–1945) 2. Jewish children. 3. Play.
4. World War, 1939–1945—Children. I. Title.
D810.J4E35 1988 87–37468
940.53'161—dc19 CIP

British Library Cataloguing in Publication date are available.

This study is dedicated to
the memory of my family
who perished in the Holocaust
It is also dedicated to my father,
Ede, and my three daughters,
Brie, Sivi, and Talia.

Contents

List of Illustrations

Preface

OCCASIONALLY AN ACCIDENT of research produces a book more engaging than the one the historian originally intended. While shifting through material for my Ph.D. dissertation, which dealt with an entirely different topic, I came across a diary from the Vilna ghetto written by Zelig Kalmanovitch. His tone was sober, but not entirely so. The passage that caught my eye concerned a playground erected around 1942 and the author's inner conflict surrounding the coexistence of games and sports and mass murder in the ghetto. In retrospect, it was quite a find, for this paragraph propelled me to look for a new dimension to the tragedy of children during the Holocaust. The Holocaust was not an unfamiliar subject to me. I grew up with its stories, but the tales of pain, suffering, death, and the fight for survival were not particularly frightening at the time. Rather, they captivated and puzzled me. I faced them with incomprehension—a sort of disbelief.

It never before dawned upon me that by being born during the Holocaust I was also a part of its history. While I was growing up, this fact seemed to possess neither special significance nor did it impart a sense of uniqueness to me. Yet in the background, in the corners of my mind, there was always a multitude of questions. Where they raised because of the painful absence of grandparents, uncles, cousins, and other relatives? Looking around me, I remember how much I missed them as a child. Maybe it was the tales my father and mother told about survival and death on the streets of wartime Budapest and in the concentration camp of Mauthausen. Perhaps it was the story of my brother who as a twelve-year old boy had the courage to jump off the train heading toward Auschwitz, while my cousin and grandmother continued their journey to the inevitable end. I listened to these accounts spellbound—gaining, subconsciously perhaps, an appreciation for history. My family also entrusted me with a special heritage—a legacy of remembering and chronicling, and I am thankful to them for the inheritance.

I consider myself fortunate to have been given the opportunity and time to write about children in the Holocaust. In writing this book there were no dull moments and no disappointments—the material I stumbled upon, tragic and fascinating as it was, had never been explored. The writing of a book, any book, is a complex and demanding task. During the process of researching and composing this work I came to appreciate this fact more and more. I was put to the test both emotionally and professionally—partly by the subject matter and partly by the realization that only a wholly interdisciplinary approach could provide a broad understanding of the Holocaust. To grasp the enormity of the tragedy and to provide a coherent picture of it, while retaining a cloak of objectivity, were most taxing challenges.

Objectivity presumes the telling of both sides of a story as evenhandedly as possible, using words sparingly and selectively. But the fate of the children in the Holocaust allows only one side. A detached language of historiography used to describe specific world events is inadequate to convey the children's story. During the review process, interestingly enough, two schools of thought clashed in evaluating this work. An American scholar voiced some apprehension that I might "sentimentalize" this topic, while European reviewers expressed admiration for the constraints exhibited throughout the analysis. The divergent views are worth pondering because they demonstrate more than differences in historiographical approach. They exemplify an inherent conflict between one who lived through the inferno (as many Europeans did, regardless of race or nationality) and the observer who concentrates only on the facts. In this situation, one can hope for no more than a delicate balance between a subconscious identification with the victims and a faithful portrayal of reality.

The many people whom I came in contact with during the course of my work were more than cooperative. I found new friends and I discovered new qualities within old friends. One is always at a loss for words to thank so many people for their scholarly and emotional support. Without their care and encouragement I would have been unable to produce this book.

From its initial beginning, I was supported by the able assistance of Adair Klein and her library staff in the Simon Wiesenthal Center of Los Angeles. These people's efforts greatly furthered my research. Miriam Novich, the curator of the Ghetto Fighters' Museum in Israel and a motivational force for remembering the Holocaust, provided me with photographic material. The chief archivist of the Leo Baeck Institute in New York, Ms. Diane R. Spielman, helped me find precious shortcuts in the maze of the "archival" world. Similar goodwill was exhibited by the archivist of the YIVO Institute of New York. Sue Benny, who heads the interlibrary loan section of California State Polytechnic University library, also worked to secure a multitude of sources.

Among the new friends and acquaintances that I made are some who are survivors of the Holocaust. In spite of their experiences, or because of them, they were willing to assist me. Their conviction that we must remember and record the atrocities of that time for future generations encouraged me to continue to write. Other friends are scholars who understood the importance of the theme of this book. They are a colorful gallery of individuals whose humanism is equal only to their dedication. I am grateful to Edza (Esther) Millich, a gracious woman, for her translations from Yiddish and Polish. Another warm human being whom I had the fortune to meet in the course of my research was Sidney Pearl. He translated a badly damaged Yiddish flyer from the Lodz ghetto. Others, such as Paul Trepman of Montreal, who sent important material for me from Canada, and Gabe Galgo of New York, also advanced my work greatly. Special thanks are due to Gabriele Silten, one of the founders of the Children Survivors of the Holocaust in southern California. She not only provided valuable recollections from her years in the camps but also proofread the final manuscript. Sybil Milton, an eminent scholar and historian of the Holocaust, provided precious assistance as well as encouragement from New York. Similar thanks are due to Dr. Judith Kestenberg, whose research into the psychological traumas of the Holocaust opened new areas of interest for me, and to Leland Holder who enhanced the quality of many of the faded photographs used in this book. A special note should be made about the assistance and encouragement of my friend Dr. Ferenc Zold. He is a humanist and a connoisseur of history and literature, and I thank him for many hours of delightful conversation and insight. There are obviously many others who were instrumental in bringing this material together—survivors of the Holocaust who granted interviews, archivists who provided me with material, and colleagues who read the manuscript. A warm thanks to them collectively.

And finally, I should devote some space to my family who sacrificed so much time and energy to enable me to research and write. The innocent blue eyes and smiles of my three beautiful daughters, Gabriella, Sivan, and Talia, often reminded me of the eyes of the millions of children who have never returned. I read in their faces, or perhaps just imagined, the same silent question: What would you have done to protect us? Following the reading of countless diaries and testimonies, I often pondered that question. I must admit that I have found no definitive answers to this tormenting question.

To thank my wife, Cynthe, for her assistance in a few words would not do justice to her role in the creation of this book. She was with me all through the research and writing, providing me with emotional support. Sometimes with a cup of coffee and sometimes with a soft word, she stood behind this undertaking at all times. More important, her sensitivity and caring provided badly needed shelter after the long readings of the harrowing tales of the Holocaust.

Children and Play in the Holocaust

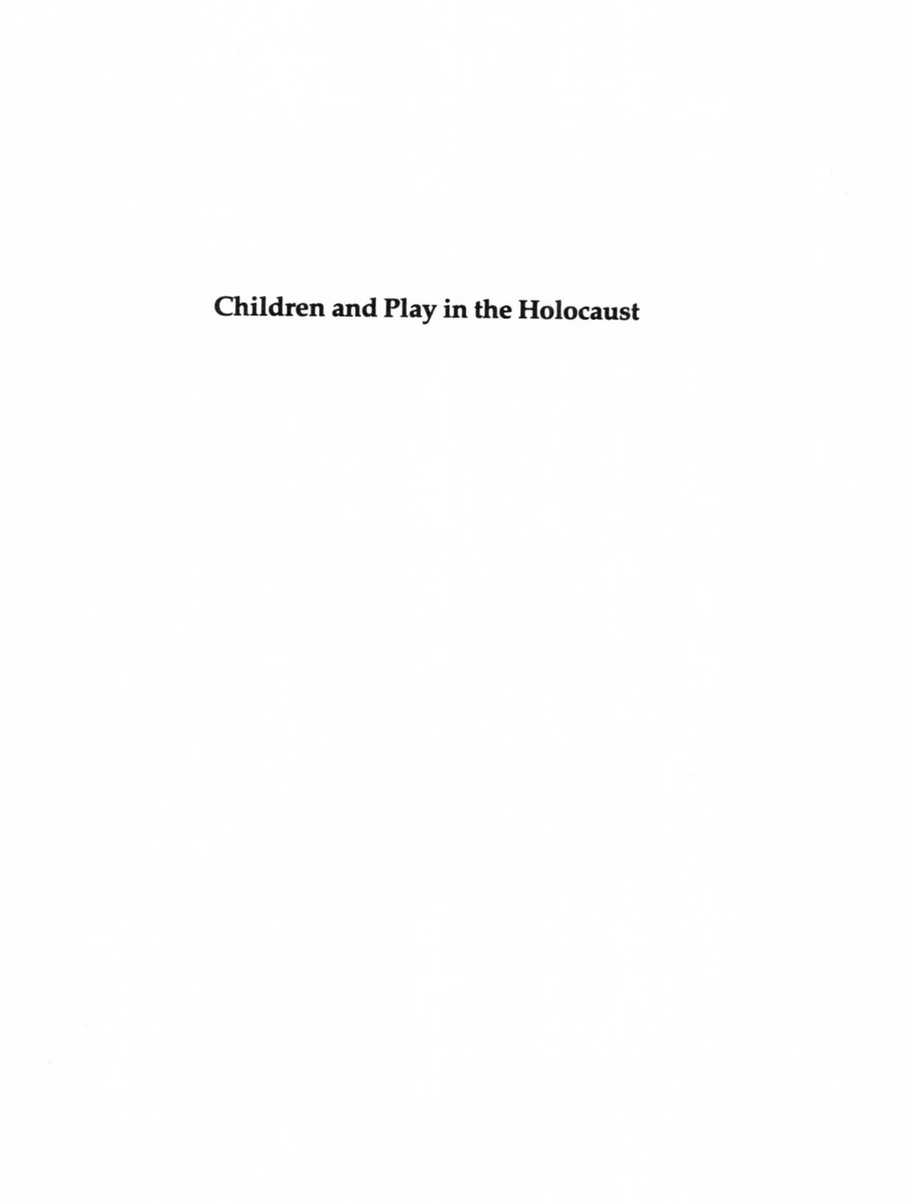

1
Prologue

"Will there be
schools and
playgrounds there,
Daddy?"

THE TRAIN SLOWLY crossed the border, picking up speed toward an unknown destination. "Still we had enough water for a while," the sole survivor of this transport later recalled in his memoirs:

> A little girl of about nine looked up at her father and said: "Will there be schools and playgrounds there, Daddy, like there are at home? Will there be lots of other children?"
>
> For a moment, indeed, the wagon was quiet, subdued by the child's shrill voice. Then her father ruffled her hair gently and said: "Yes darling. There'll be schools and playgrounds . . . everything you want."[1]

It seems likely that this little girl never realized, even after the long march toward the tall chimneys, that for her there would be no more playtime. In fact, neither the diarist, nor the father, nor the little girl could have had an inkling of Majdanek where there was no place for children and where the chimneys belching black smoke signified, diabolically, the end of the road.

This book is not only about this single child; it is also about millions of children who all wanted to play, and who did, perhaps, play for a short moment, but who died. And it is about others who, although they survived, had to grow up fast in a hostile world. Through the medium of play, this book puts faces, deeds, and words to the incomprehensible numbers of the murdered. It chronicles the play activities of the young, the attitudes and view of adult society toward these activities, and the desperate attempts of the adults to salvage a familiar world, re-create a sense of normalcy through play, and construct islands of culture that would insulate the young from a suddenly savage world. It also throws a sharp light on how these activities were perceived by the youngsters themselves and on the curious dimensions that play assumed in their lives.

My main theme deals primarily with experiences in the Holocaust, but the study offers also a certain universality, for it addresses as well the basic theorem of play under adverse circumstances, under stress, and under inhuman conditions, the conditions of children in war. As any historian or survivor could testify, this topic is a complex and emotional one. After all, hardly ever has a subject proved so gripping as the Holocaust. It confronts us with clear-cut yet unanswerable questions about our humanity, values, and capacity for suffering. It also defies in its scope, number, and magnitude the human imagination. Hans Frank, one of the most notorious war criminals tried in Nuremberg, admitted in a moment of repentance: "You cannot call it just a crime—crime is too mild a word for it. Stealing is a crime; killing one man is a crime—but this—this is just beyond human imagination!"[2]

Estimates of the number of Jewish children who died between the years 1939 and 1945 vary. Some historians put the number around a million, which, compared to the six million total, seems unduly conservative. One cannot ignore the fact that the fertility rate of Eastern Jewry, the primary victims of the Nazi genocide, was much higher than that of the West—in Poland alone, children were one-fourth of the population. It is also true that the chance of survival for the young was the lowest among all groups targeted for extermination. These two factors suggest a much higher number of children victims—close to one and a half million would be more accurate. For Western minds, trained to comprehend the world more in quantitative than conceptual terms, over one million children murdered is perhaps too shocking to digest—the power of this number itself numbs the mind. It is perhaps easier to comprehend the magnitude of the disaster if one considers that of fifteen thousand children who passed through Theresienstadt (Terezin)—euphemistically called a ghetto but in reality a concentration camp—only an estimated one hundred survived.[3] Indeed, the percentage of Jewish children who survived the Nazi genocide was the lowest of any age group that came through the Holocaust. Of course, these are some of the bare statistics, and they obviously give only an incomplete picture. The suffering of these children, even with all the accounts at our disposal, is impossible to comprehend.

In the totality of the Holocaust children's play represents only a limited cross section of human experiences. Nevertheless, a study of it brings forward many of the same dilemmas and issues that are inherent in writing about any aspect of this tragic period.[4] One of the most fundamental realizations is that, in spite of an insulating distance that time and space can offer, it is almost impossible to write about the Holocaust impersonally and it is even harder to do so about children. The pain and agony of millions of victims have left an ingrained shock which the rational historical approach can never fully deal with. Lawrence Langer's words are poignantly convincing when he admits that "the monstrous inhumanity of Auschwitz has a way of asserting its presence despite the imagination's desire to transcend it."[5]

Also, children's play and the Holocaust confront the untrained observer with a perplexing contradiction. The question of whether mass murder and play could exist side by side was as acutely pertinent to people then as it is today—in the Vilna ghetto, for example, the central issue occupying the minds of a large segment of the population was that "a graveyard is no place for merriment." Mass murder signifies the ultimate evil while play, at least in popular imagination, speaks of a measure of innocence and happiness. Indeed, at first glance the abyss between these two seems unbridgeable. An amalgamation of brutal killing and play is disconcerting and abrupt, but no more so than the other bizarre absurdities of the Holocaust universe. A painting by Malvina Schalkova of children playing with the funeral hearse at Theresienstadt combines the extremes and provides a shocking yet apt metaphor of the children's place in the process of destruction. Whereas the hearse represents annihilation, the children are in the life-affirming act of playing, embodying a tenacious will and principle of existence.

Perhaps the most mystifying thing about play is that, on the one hand, it is supposed to be disengaged from reality in a variety of ways, while at the same time it is credited with a great number of useful real-life functions. The concept of play was defined by one of the earliest play theorists, Johan Huizinga, as a "free activity standing quite consciously outside ordinary life as being not serious."[6] Although his definition presents a highly romanticized view of child's play, it reflects common beliefs. It is not surprising that the word *play* in the popular imagination conjures a careless world of frolic and joy, an activity void of purpose and rationale—a picture that is hardly compatible with the horrid world of the Warsaw ghetto:

> The streets resound with the futile screams of children dying of hunger. They whine, beg, sing, lament, and tremble in the cold, without underwear, without clothes, without shoes. . . .
>
> Children swollen from hunger, deformed, semi-conscious; children who are perfectly adults, somber and tired of living at age five.[7]

It is almost impossible to wholly reconcile the paradox of these two worlds. It is unlikely that any book will be able to resolve completely this conflict between children's play and the evil of this abysmal and depraved period. The only rationale that might suggest a solution to this dilemma, and evidence will support this on the following pages, is that children's play was not divorced from reality. In fact, play behavior was reflective of it, and it articulated skills for survival as well.[8]

As in every area of life, the nature, intensity, and range of human experiences of each individual are the causal function of time, space, and environment. A clarifying comment on the substantial differences that distinguished various institutions of the extermination mechanism is in order here. Ghettos were particularly characteristic institutions of Eastern Europe; in the West transit camps served the Nazi regime as collection points for deportation eastward. In Poland and the Baltic States a relatively homogenous Jewish population was more discernible and thus was segregated with relative ease from the native population. Within the stages of descent toward the final destruction, ghettos and camps were for many only the initial and, perhaps, the "mildest" places of incarceration. Yet, even within various ghettos there were degrees of severity and differing reasons for their existence. The customary meaning of the word *ghetto* itself is inadequate to convey the true nature of the Nazi version of this establishment. In that era it meant something quite different from the concentration of a certain number of individuals; it meant the slow death of thousands through hunger, forced labor and disease. Transit camps, on the other hand, served for the collection of Jews in Western Europe—France, Holland, and Italy, where the Jewish people differed very little from the rest of the surrounding population. Established camps for forced labor constituted the next step, and extermination camps, the final step in the complete annihilation of European Jewry. Again, the severity and purpose of these two "institutions" set them apart from each other. It is inevitable, then, that where one was incarcerated had far-reaching ramifications on the prisoner's experiences and chances of survival. Benedikt Kautsky, a prisoner himself, offers this explanation: "When you talk about a concentration camp, it's not enough to give merely its name. . . . Even when you're talking about the same period of time, prisoners in the same camp lived as if on different planets."[9]

Play is far from a frivolous activity. It may take place in even the most hostile environments. Reflecting the atrocities, or perhaps in response to them, there could be some unique dimensions of a child's play in the Holocaust that might not be immediately apparent to the casual observer and that our civilization is not always willing or able to grasp. An ability to play, of course, promised no guarantee of surviving. Indeed, the innocence of the young and their will to create a sane world, or to cope with a convoluted one, does not detract from the evil. Rather their play helps to provide a stark contrast and illumination of its depth and complexity. It is an encapsulation of a real-life drama on the cognitive level of a child. Here we can find, also, the major dividing line between children's and adult play. It might be justifiably argued that adult sports, games, and recreational activities had lost their traditional meaning in Nazi Europe. A shift from the elation and joy of human action and mastery of one's body and mind for adults was abrupt and unavoidable. One sign of this transformation is the vignette of a fifty-five-year-old woman, red cabbage rubbed into her cheeks to give them healthy color, literally running the race of her life, while being timed with a stopwatch by an SS doctor, because those who came in last were taken away and liquidated. "This was the true contest," one survivor recalled in a documentary novel. "With your stomach turning and your breath thin, you run—beneath the throb of the lying music—for your golden life." The other marker of the times is the singing and merriment, "a hectic straining that expressed a preoccupation with the few pleasures the ghetto could offer, a frantic wish to live fast and dangerously before the end came."[10]

Children's play is governed by unique sets of rules that are not always tamed by adult rationalization. It can retain, even in the most adverse moments, a modicum of "innocence." Yet portraying it only as "levity," 'frivolity," or "frolic" is a grave misrepresentation of its true nature. Indeed, one of the mysteries of this tragic epoch was that the children played (if only for a fleeting moment), dreamed of freedom, and tried to understand a hostile world where the most frightening element of the irrational was its rationality. One of the givens in the study of play is that when a child is at play, he or she is engaged in an experience that is inherently meaningful—even if its meaning and rationale are not immediately obvious to the child. In Huizinga's words, again, "play is a thing by itself. The play-concept as such is of higher order than is seriousness. For seriousness seeks to exclude play, whereas play can very well include seriousness."[11]

Yet, Huizinga's point is valid only in normal circumstances. The Nazi period was a time that transcended human comprehension with its terror and cruelty. The Holocaust, with its extreme physical and psychological pressures, was to have such a profound effect upon society that "seriousness" often defined play. Play, at the same time, reflected, inevitably, the surrounding "seriousness." Ethological observations have demonstrated that the play behavior of children is markedly dependent on the play setting in which it is taking place and that environmental factors rather than "personality differences" are the major determinants of formulating this behavior.[12]

This observation seems, in turn, to reinforce one of the recurring themes in modern scholarly literature which puts forward the view that play, games, and sport can be seen as a "microcosm" of the larger society. The nature of play and its organization, goals, function, and structure provide revealing clues about ghetto society. Beyond that, an analysis of play and the role that individuals and the Jewish community attributed to it and envisaged for it might document times and mentalities in the Holocaust as richly and vividly as political, social, and economic analyses can. Whatever validity one assigns to this interpretation of play in society and history, it is glaringly evident from surviving descriptions that play activities in ghettos and camps, and the attitudes associated with them, reflected the historical, cultural, economic, and psychological milieu. Concurrently, they also mirrored the dominant values of a traumatized society pushed to the brink of mental and physical destruction. The organization of play pursuits for the young could only occupy a limited place, but it was a significant one, and the importance of its position shows that the business of play is more than a temporary intrusion into history.

THE COMPLEXITY OF human existence was especially evident during the destruction process because the inevitable instinct for survival predominated over any other endeavors. Before their final ordeal, people everywhere—in ghettos, camps, and hiding—responded with a stubborn determination to outlast their executioners. One of the manifestations of this grim will, negating all conventional assumption, was the organization of play activities for the traumatized youth of ghettos and camps. These pursuits were turned into an enterprise of survival, a defense for sanity, and a demonstration of psychological defiance. In general, the care of children in the ghettos lay outside the direct interest of the occupation authorities, who as a rule did not prohibit these endeavors. Indirectly, however, the Germans had the ability to control effectively all aspects of life within the ghettos or camps for they were the ultimate masters in providing or denying vital supplies to the Jewish communities. Carrying on play and recreational pursuits for the young required inventiveness as well as sacrifice. The desperate attempts of the community, in ghettos and even in concentration camps, to reestablish, often through play and games, the equilibrium of the young's moral, spiritual, and physical universe demonstrate an appreciation that play activities have importance beyond their recreational values. From an adult point of view they also assumed dimensions not normally associated with children's play.

Amidst the suffering, hunger, and extermination, we are hard pressed to place play and games in a context of mystical experience, conveying eternal verities or embodying cosmic principles that have been attributed to the human suffering and martyrdom during the Holocaust in general. Indeed, the literature of this era was, until recently, preoccupied with these complex issues. Somehow the everyday life, with its mundane or dramatic moments, has escaped the attention of many. Yet the questions of how people handled the burden of existence and how they coped with the terror all around them are as tantalizing and difficult as any philosophical truism. One must conclude that the art of life in the Holocaust was not easier than that of death. Only now, perhaps as a consequence of the distancing perspective of elapsed time, works on art, music, and photography in the Holocaust have begun to surface. Indeed, the central focus of these new endeavors moved away from the concept of the Holocaust itself and examined instead its ramifications on the human psyche, behavior, and responses. This transition is a most important process, for finding answers to how humans existed in "hell on earth," as a writer put it, is at least as important as finding eternal verities. These answers can provide us with some explanation of human responses to horrors in our present world. The purpose of this book, then, transcends the Holocaust and attempts to find a rationale for children's play in war everywhere. My study relies on the recognition that within the concentric circles of hell there is also an intricate spectrum of life from which the descent to death is the last release in a tortuous series of stages.

The belief that life must go on, in spite of its wretchedness, held as much power as the fear of extermination. During the Holocaust, makeshift playgrounds were erected, "Children's Month" proclaimed, chess tournaments, play days, and sports contests organized, and sometimes even concerts and many theatrical performances held. These actitives were rational and necessary, even in a world that was not always governed by rational rules. They merely confirmed one of the deepest instincts in the human mind—the need to establish a defensive perimeter by every means available, especially at a time when the range of action is severely limited. At best, then a study of the play activities of the young and the role they had in sheltering children from realities, heightening the morale and self-esteem of an utterly demoralized people, and fostering a will to survive gives a human dimension to a tragic era.

Although the majority of the sources for this book describe the tale of Eastern European Jewry in Nazi ghettos and concentration camps, in its universality the book transcends historical periods or geographical areas. It reflects, indeed, the universality of children's suffering and their responses in war. The systematic and cynical killing of millions of people is shocking enough, but the wanton and savage extermination of children and the ferocity with which they were treated before their final ordeal are unmatched in history. The suffering and inarticulate cry of these children cannot be hidden; their pleas for life resonate on the pages of diaries and in the memories of those who survived.

Extant diaries and documents are curious remnants of a doomed civilization. In them, the faint glimmers of hope for a better future and the lasting belief in the basic goodness of the world often pierce through the darkness of this period of depravity and misery. It is true that these sources cannot reflect accurately the experiences of all the millions of victims, but they testify rather eloquently not only to the horror but also to the rare moments of joy. They offer precious information about the opinions and views of people who subconsciously perceived the immediacy of the end but tenaciously clung to their humanity. Their determination is nowhere more apparent than in the words of Mira Jakubowicz, a supervisor of a ghetto playground, whose decision to stay with her pupils sealed her fate: "I consider it my duty to remain here in the ghetto [Warsaw] . . . Don't you see how much they need love and care and laughter? They have so little time left."[13]

One must recognize that describing children's play was not, understandably, a priority for camp inmates or ghetto dwellers. Many of the diaries and documents were composed under the most trying circumstances, and questions of life and survival imposed their own censure on subjects not immediately pertinent to existence. The writings resonate with the sorrow and anguish of a community that had few illusions about its own fate. These same sources, however, left us a marvelous legacy of descriptions of children at play and their behavior, reflecting a faint belief in a distant future. They serve as a vote for survival against overwhelming odds, in which play, like all other human endeavors, had an important role.

Although the systematic study of human responses to mass murder is a relatively recent phenomenon, its literature is rapidly growing. The Holocaust and its effect on society have never been fully comprehended or explained, and it is perhaps too much to expect that full comprehension or explanation is possible. Because much less has been written about children's experiences, an understanding of them will probably be even less definitive. Only a precious few survived to recount their harrowing tales and they have left very little literary legacy. It is primarily to an occasional diary that we must turn for testimony of the specific nature of their tragedy.

A similarly glaring void confronts us on the subject of children's behavior and emotional responses in drastically altered living conditions, and this lack of documentation does not apply only to the Holocaust. Play itself as a mediating medium has never been examined and studied in this context. And, one might add, laboratory experiments that take place in well controlled and artificially created environments provide very little basis for sweeping and definitive conclusions. Play as such is a unique and creative manifestation of an innate energy characteristic of humans and animals alike. Although play's function, effects, and rationale have been studied more extensively, its inner source and motivation remain an enigma, a topic for conjecture at best. Is it an animalistic instinct without purpose, or a subconscious urge preparing people for adult life? Or is it even a means by which a society transmits its culture? These questions are rhetorical in the purest sense because, although many social and psychological theorists have grappled with these same issues, they have found, as yet, no conclusive explanations. The best one can suggest, and this is the message of this book, is that play is a subset of life in which one can rehearse for the serious business of adaptation—even for the ultimate adaptation of accepting death and suffering by enacting them in a play setting. But in the same context, play also succeeds in creating an arrangement in which a child can practice behavior eminently directed for survival.

Many books, perhaps thousands, have been written about the origin and consequences of the Holocaust. It has been dissected and then reconstructed with historical and philosophical logic and analytic detail, without, as one can see, final and definitive answers. Although this study cannot and will not attempt to provide an answer either, through an interdisciplinary analysis a sharper sketch of life in the Holocaust may emerge. Indeed, for a clearer understanding of the Holocaust an interdisciplinary approach is a must. An amalgamation of the disciplines of history, psychology, and anthropology can only enhance a fragmented and incomplete historical reality. Also, with the combination of the two concepts of play and the Holocaust, this book offers a novel and unfamiliar dimension to the tragedy of European Jewry in general and of children in particular. It will also provide some explanation of play as a means for social and psychological adaptation in times of duress and adversity. It is to be hoped that it will not be the last word on these subjects, for writing about them is a must. "Everything must be said. Everything!" a survivor recently remarked. "Yet, we perhaps never will be able to say it all."

2
The Child in the Holocaust

"No one will ever
be able to forget
those children's voices"

THE STUDY OF CHILDREN's play in the Holocaust is not a trivialization of a tragedy unparalleled in human history. The contrast between children's play and the horror of the times not only brings into a starker focus the children's hunger, suffering, and demise but also elucidates the enormity of the crime. After all, the Second World War introduced a new dimension, a shockingly sordid idea, into the history of modern warfare. It was the first time the annihilation of a defenseless civilian population, involving a multitude of nationalities, became the explicit object of destruction. It has become evident that the perpetrators initiated and carried out their campaign of extermination on such a scale that no rational mind can fathom its magnitude. One of the architects of this policy, Hans Frank, who repented on the eve of his execution, looked back in awe on Hitler's success in "reducing murder to mass production!"

It has often been suggested that these efforts were based on racial ideology as much as on misguided military necessity. We have to accept, however, one thing that is beyond dispute; among the children, only Jews and Gypsies were singled out as a special category for mass destruction. "They are the first to be exterminated," a grieving ghetto historian exclaimed. "Except for Pharoah, who ordered the newborn Hebrew babes thrown into the river Nile, this is unprecedented in Jewish history." One might add that it is unprecedented throughout human history. The experiences and final fate of Jewish children in this turbulent period comprises, inevitably, only a part of the agony and overall tragedy of the Holocaust. Yet, children, swept up by the winds of terror, became perhaps the most explicit targets of destruction from the early stages of the Nazi action. A relentless war was waged within a war, and its particular victims—children and youth—were forced through a special hell. The story of their martyrdom is, indeed, the most shocking and darkest chapter of Western civilization. While these words are uncompromisingly strong, the sheer number of victims alone, ignoring for a moment their unquantifiable suffering and pain, is a good indicator of the magnitude of their destruction. One cannot discard the fact that while the hate and terror directed against Jews was greater than that against any other ethnic or racial group, it became singularly more brutal, if a degree could be attached to terror, when children were concerned. The most shocking to all was the compulsively automatic behavior, almost detached, of the conquerors. A witness in the Eichmann trial, Noah Zabludowicz, recalled an act of incomprehensible cruelty:

> Once I saw an SS officer in Ciechanow politely asking a Jewish mother in the street to let him try to appease her crying baby. With incredulity in her eyes and with trembling hands the woman delivered the infant, whereupon the Nazi smashed the baby's small head on the sharp edge of the curbstone. . . . [1]

One may question why—if the central theme of this book is children's play—scenes like this and similar ones are discussed? This question, in light of the hundreds of publications that have been dedicated to the depiction of the atrocities and inhumanity of the Holocaust, is justified. However, before we even approach the main topic—the analysis and understanding of children's play—the etching of a sharp picture of the milieu surrounding the children and shaping their perception and responses is absolutely essential. After all, their play, just like all human experiences, was reflective of and governed by societal, psychological, and economic conditions of the society in which they took place.

In examining surviving documents and reading testimonies, one can easily detect a clear pattern in German actions. The military precision in carrying out their extermination plans and the frightful detachment with which SS officers and even civilian authorities conducted them betray analytical thinking and meticulous planning. In the Nazi scheme of things there was a special design for Jewish children. The Germans' logic was based primarily on the notion that Jews, including their children, must be eradicated as a matter of ideological necessity. The treatment of the young in ghettos and in concentration camps was a by-product of this belief; after the full exploitation of the population, the whole race must disappear, especially pregnant women and the young, the "biological roots of the Jewish people." Thus, in keeping with the abysmal animosity toward this particular racial group, irrational and pathological as it was, the solution of the "Jewish question" proceeded on a well-planned path.

The painfully familiar outline of this process entailed two geographically and chronologically overlapping alternatives. Both contained frightful consequences for the children. In the first one, the final ordeal commenced and ended with a singular act, the outright slaughter of all or a major part of the Jewish inhabitants of an entire city or geographic area. The second alternative overlapped, chronologically, with the first one. Concurrently with the outright extermination process, the tentacles of a vast network of ghettos and concentration camps spread through Europe. German plans were also governed, after all, by economic dictates for the exploitation of the civilian population in the conquered countries. Although it will be noted later in more detail, one must add that their concentration into ghettos and camps was preceded by, or coincided with, restrictive legislation on civil liberties, social and cultural segregation, and economic disfranchisement.

Nazism was more than an abstract ideology. It was a system with ramifications. Because Jewish children were considered "a danger for the security of the state," their future was sealed from the early stages of the occupation. For the SS the identity of their victims was an abstraction. The fate of these children and the clear, cold, and calculated Nazi design of systematically destroying them (insofar as language can reflect it) was summed up frightfully eloquently and succinctly by the SS officer Otto Ohlendorf, commander of one of the extermination squads. During his trial at Nuremberg in 1947 he matter-of-factly testified that "this order [for the killing of the young] did not only try to achieve a temporary security but also a permanent security, for the children were people who would grow up and, surely, being the children of parents who had been killed, would constitute a danger no smaller than that of the parents."[2]

As a direct consequence of this policy, an untold number of children shared their parents' fate and were executed during 1941 and 1942 by subsequent waves of the Einsatzgruppen [mobile killing units] activity. These massacres affected, for the most part, Jews in the Baltic States and occupied areas of the Soviet Union. Although it has been estimated that by the end of 1942 more than a million Jews had been murdered by mobile killing squads, no one has ever ventured to calculate the number of children among these early victims. The methods employed by the SS, the cruelty of the perpetrators, and the dignity and pleas of the victims have been described often by both the executioners and the victims. There were distinct executions of children who were collected specifically and taken to predug trenches where they were shot. As early as the summer of 1943, three SS men stood trial in front of a Soviet tribunal in the liberated town of Charkov for killing the civilian population of this area. Among their victims had been batches of Jewish children, their ages ranging from six to twelve. "I drove the children to the brink of the ditch," one of the participants testified, " where another SS man stood. . . . He shot them with his submachine gun and, then, with the tip of his boot kicked them into the ditch. The children knew what to expect and attempted to run away. They beseeched the executioners: 'Sir, I am scared! —Sir, I would like to live, don't shoot me!' "[3]

These descriptions are graphically gruesome, but the history of the Holocaust rarely presents light moments. If they do not give the full extent and scope of the destruction, they at least provide a clear picture of its nature. The campaign of mass shooting was only a partial answer to the "Jewish Question." As in all complex solutions, it was felt necessary to employ a multitude of methods and tactics. In line with the Nazi plan of reducing the Jewish population was the forced reduction of the fertility rate through segregation of the sexes, marriage bans, and compulsory abortion. These methods had an obsessive grip on Nazi functionaries who subscribed to a raw Darwinism of promoting "racially superior" Aryan elements and the simultaneous destruction of "racially inferior" nationalities. To provide some respectability, these programs were dressed in a scientific cloak, as were so many of Germany's irrational activities, but when stripped of their false clothing, they became no more than a barbarian form of population control. For instance, in ghetto Siaulaui, Lithuania, decrees were posted notifying women that forced abortions would take place within a period of several weeks. When this policy did not produce the expected results, the SS proclaimed the death penalty for childbirth, for the mother, the infant, and the whole family:

> The time is over, it is the last minute! The 15th of August is not far! Remember Jewish women, after that time no births will be allowed in the ghetto hospital. Remember, after the 15th births will be forbidden even in private homes. A strict examination of private dwellings will be conducted. Physicians, midwives, and nurses will be forbidden to assist Jewish women. In case of insubordination, all will be punished with utmost severity. Do not forget the danger you might bring upon yourself or your family! We are warning you for the last time![4]

This effort to subvert the basic instinct of survival showed itself as one further product of sordid minds, but the rhythm of life, convoluted and grim as it was, could not be stopped by decrees alone. Extant diaries bring proof that clandestine marriage ceremonies were performed and that children were born secretly. Induced abortion, however, was not the final word in the Nazi scheme of population control. Security forces or their native hirelings killed pregnant women, infants, and all children who were not able to work.

Many children died en route to the concentration camps, and those who survived were eliminated almost immediately by whatever means possible, for they obstructed, in the German view, the working routine in the camps. Besides, in the words of the former commandant of Auschwitz, Rudolf Hoess: "Children of tender years were invariably exterminated since by reason of their youth they were unable to work." An inmate in her writings categorized the children into four groups: those gassed immediately upon arrival; those murdered in their mother's womb or immediately after birth; those born in the camp who were left alive (a rare occurrence); and those who were tall enough to pass as adults. Quite often pregnant women were sent directly either to the gas chamber or to the hospital for forced abortion. It is little wonder that in the Auschwitz/Birkenau extermination complex, at least until the end of 1943, only one Jewish child was to be found (in the Women's Camp).

The situation in Buchenwald differed very little from that of Auschwitz/Birkenau. "One day I saw a boy of four, the saddest character I had ever come across, abnormal in his physique, behaviour and speech," a fourteen-year-old boy recorded in his diary. "He staggered along like some weak, wounded animal and uttered cries in German-Polish-Yiddish gibberish. 'That,' I was told, 'is the kid they keep hiding from the SS. His father brought him here. . . . Every time there is an inspection they gag the poor devil and tuck him away underneath the floorboards. What a life!' "[5]

Auschwitz/Birkenau was, by all accounts, the epitome of a death camp, but it was not alone with its atrocities—even relatively humane camps had their own psychological torments. The occupying authorities initiated periodic sweeps in ghettos and labor camps as well. In well-orchestrated raids called *Kinderreinigung* or *Kinderaktion*, pregnant women and young children were systematically carted off to extermination centers to be gassed or killed by mass shooting, and there was very little chance to escape. Neither the serene mountains of Le Souterraine in France nor the decrepit ghettos of the East could provide a safe haven for the hunted because the hunters' hatred knew no national boundaries. French gendarmes, Ukrainian soldiers, Lithuanian partisans, and the SS masters themselves often cooperated in the capture of a handful of children.

The example of the small and picturesque French village near Lyon is instructive of these Nazi methods. On April 6, 1944, forty-four children were suddenly rounded up in the children's home in the small and serene village of Izieu. Moving quickly, the Gestapo was able to surprise the small colony. The children were thrown on the tracks "like packages," a villager later recalled. "In the village everybody liked them . . . they were children." Only one child was set free because he was not Jewish. We know now that his release meant life for him, because the remaining forty-three were hastily deported to Auschwitz and dispatched, immediately, to the gas chambers. A thousand miles away from Lyon, in Plaszow, a camp near Cracow, similar scenes were enacted during a Kinderaktion. The place itself was a combination labor and concentration camp and a few desperate parents had succeeded in smuggling in and hiding a handful of children. The children themselves understood their precarious situation and made every effort to blend into the prison population and not to obstruct the normal routine of the camp. A documentary novel by Thomas Keneally based on survivors' recollections re-creates well the heart-rending atmosphere and scenes of the day of the raid in the summer of 1944. The action was named, of all things, Die Gesundheitsaktion [the Health Action]. Indeed, the cynicism with which the SS officers planned and accomplished their grisly task finds parallel only in other stories of their cruelty. The people assembled on the children's playground while the tearing away of nearly three hundred children from their trembling parents was accompanied by blaring loudspeakers, which played a sentimental song called "Mammi, kauf mir ein Pferdchen" ("Mummy, buy me a pony").[6]

It has been argued that the human mind has an inexhaustible capacity for absorbing atrocity. The Holocaust often presents us with degrees of barbarity that probe even our own humanity. A description by a twelve-year-old boy of the destruction of a maternity ward in the Lodz ghetto, where his sister had just given birth to a baby girl, not only typifies these methods, but also exemplifies the shock and trauma of a child learning about infanticide:

> Then as the next group of patients was being escorted to a waiting truck, we saw Esther. . . . She was pale and frightened as she stood there in her pink nightgown. . . . Soon the truck drove off and we knew we could never see our beloved Esther again. . . . There was silence for a moment. No one could figure what was going to happen next. . . .
>
> Suddenly, two Germans appeared in an upper story window and pushed it open. Seconds later a naked baby was pushed over the ledge and dropped to its death directly into the truck below. We were in such shock that at first few of us believed it was actually a live, newborn baby. . . .

> The SS seemed to enjoy this bloody escapade. . . . the young SS butcher rolled up his rifle sleeve and caught the very next infant on his bayonet. The blood of the infant flowed down the knife onto the murderer's arm . . . [7]

NOT ALL CHILDREN were killed outright. The postponement, however, was not evidence of generosity, for those who were not immediately murdered were provided only a brief reprieve from death. The delay in carrying out the destruction was underlined by a systematic starvation, which especially targeted the children. Beyond the constant physical and psychological terror, occupation administrations confiscated Jewish property, introduced arm-bands and yellow patches, and initiated expulsions of millions from rural areas or small settlements to large population centers or concentration camps. This last step signified the actual ghettoization of millions of people.

German administrators initially experimented with ghettos in 1939, though it was not until the spring of 1940 that the first full-fledged ghetto came into existence in Lodz. Soon afterward, half a million people were incarcerated in Warsaw, the largest ghetto of all. Within a year, small and large ghettos, camps, and Jewish "quarters," amounting to hundreds of establishments, quickly mushroomed into a Nazi empire. Sprawling across the map of Europe, they were uniquely sinister institutions; ghettos, as Goebbels himself deemed to define them, became "death boxes" *(Todekiste)*. Abraham Levin, a teacher in Warsaw, noted in his diary on May 18, 1942, "we are not able to enjoy nature, from the beautiful world of the Creator. We are languishing in a prison that no one has experienced in the history of mankind."[8] Socially and economically uprooted and psychologically depressed, the large number of ghetto inhabitants, especially millions of children, faced the bleakest prospect of survival. Many of them were orphaned or abandoned, and their struggle to exist was not only hampered by cold, hunger, and disease but also by the unrelenting cruelty and determination with which the SS officers worked for their demise. Starvation, was, undoubtedly, the most merciless tormentor of the children in the ghetto. Hunger subjugated the ghetto mentally and physically, destroying the normal rhythm of existence, accelerating aging, and withering its victims. "The most painful change has affected the faces." a contemporary exclaimed, "faces worn down to the bones by misery, lack of food, vitamins, air and exercise; faces disfigured by overwhelming worries, anxieties, mishaps, sufferings, and illness."[9]

The year 1941 saw, in Warsaw and other ghettos, tens of thousands of children fall victim to hunger and disease. The catastrophic dislocation of a

1. Very young children playing jacks in the Lodz ghetto, 1940–41. The yellow star was mandatory for everyone. From the Archives of the Simon Wiesenthal Center, Los Angeles, Calif.

large percentage of Eastern European Jewry created a favorable climate for the German plans of destruction. In the Warsaw ghetto alone there were over 150,000 refugees, and this number represented close to one-third of the entire population. Most of them were housed in makeshift dwellings with broken down sanitary facilities, without heat and elementary amenities. One-third of these refugees were under fifteen. "I have visited a refugee home," reports Mary Berg in her diary. "It is a desolate building. The former walls of the separate rooms have been broken down to form large halls; there are no conveniences; the plumbing has been destroyed. . . . On the floor I saw half naked, unwashed children lying listlessly."[10]

The refugees' inability to provide their children with the barest necessities became one of the most tragic aspects of their sad existence. The quick crumbling of the protective walls around the child manifested itself not only in the rapid dissolution of community ties, especially among the refugees, but also in the destruction of the basic organizational unit of society, the nuclear family. Deliberate Nazi policies tore families apart by deportation, execution, and consignment of fathers to labor camps. In every ghetto, the steadily increasing number of children without parental supervision, and orphans without any support, provides us with a clear testimony of this tragic development. The most traumatic and damaging psychological experience for a child is a feeling of losing the close ties with parents and family. Lost completely in an alien and forlorn environment, many children lived and died on the streets. "These are children who were orphaned when both parents died either in wanderings or in the typhus epidemic," wrote Chaim Kaplan in Warsaw. "Every morning you will see their little bodies frozen to death in the ghetto streets. It has become a customary sight." In January 1942 a welfare report summarized the state of refugees in the Warsaw ghetto: "Hunger, sickness, and want are their constant companions, and death is the only visitor in their homes."[11]

While hunger physically destroyed the body, the ghetto itself subjugated the children. Living conditions, exacerbated by congestion and crowding beyond description, took their toll on the children's spirits. There was no escape from the narrow, dirty streets, dilapidated tenement houses, and the swarming multitude. From the Warsaw ghetto a girl wrote: "My ears are filled with the deafening clamor of crowded streets and cries of people dying on the sidewalks." For many, the ghetto meant not only the deprivation of physical freedom and of bare economic isolation. "We are cut off from the world of books," a diarist noted. "Nothing reaches us, the creations of the human mind are not permitted to enter our prison. Not only groceries and industrial goods, but cultural products as well have to be smuggled into the ghetto."[12]

Restrictions were introduced into every area of human existence. And, for the children, the psychological repression was as painful as the absence of food or heat, for it shackled the human spirit. With frightful thoroughness and diabolic insight, Germans banned the Jewish population from parks, public gardens, river banks, swimming pools, and all other places of entertainment—this decree was always a prominent policy of the occupation authorities everywhere. "With intentional foresight," a mother in the Warsaw ghetto recorded, "not one park, not one playground or public garden was included in the area [picked for the ghetto]." A chronicler from the ghetto of Lodz had a similar impression: "The Ghetto, with its approximately 85,000 inhabitants, is probably the only city in the world without any, or almost any flowers." There were children who throughout their short lives never saw an amusement park or even a garden.[13]

Simultaneously with these policies of restriction, the educational systems in almost all ghettos became victims of similar decrees. With one swipe of the pen, schools were outlawed and Jewish learning, specifically that of

2. The death of a child in the Warsaw ghetto, 1940–41. Courtesy of the Ghetto Fighters' Museum, Israel.

children, was forbidden under the threat of death, mostly in Poland and the Baltic States. Although it took almost two years and countless petitions, Germans at last permitted a limited reopening of the school system on the elementary and trade-school levels. In Kovno schools functioned for only a few months and never reopened again. On the whole, only a small minority of the youth could attend the newly opened schools either because of the Jewish communal authorities' lack of resources or because many of the youngsters were the sole breadwinners for entire familes.

The immediate consequences of these edicts were felt by thousands of children who roamed aimlessly, "exposed to the demoralizing inflluence of the street." Isaiah Trunk, an official in the Lodz ghetto, mournfully remarked that no place remained for the children: "they are excluded from homes, because of the crowding, from the schools, because of the edicts, and only the streets provide them with free space." The Germans went also to great lengths to exclude Jews completely from the German sphere of culture. Nazi decrees banned in the ghettos and camps the performances of all literary, musical, and other art works attributable to Aryan writers, composers, and artists. Although some variation existed in enforcing these rules —and because there was a definite confusion as to who was Aryan—the same general method of exclusion was practiced everywhere. To provide one example, in Westerbork several works were first banned from Jewish performances because the composers were considered Aryan. Later, however, the Germans discovered a "blemish" in these composers' family background and their music became acceptable. Although in Holland the Germans acted with discretion and circumspection, in Poland the cultural censure included other art forms. A bewildered observer wrote in the spring of 1942 that orders were issued banning "any literary, art, or musical work produced or composed by an Aryan." In the same year, the ghetto's symphony orchestra was closed down for the transgression of playing Beethoven. In Lodz and Vilna no such ban existed, but when musical instruments were confiscated, music and dancing were effectively eliminated from the ghetto altogether.[14]

Petty and absurd as these restrictions may seem, they heightened the sense of isolation and imprisonment. Thousands of children, once vibrant, creative and industrious, became walled in and sealed off from the surrounding world. The deprivation of freedom was hard to bear and it was acutely felt by them. A fourteen-year-old boy from the small village of Krajno in rural Poland recorded his anguish in simple words: "If only there were freedom then everything would be fine." Another boy in Vilna had similar thoughts upon moving in the ghetto: "I feel that I have been robbed, my freedom is being robbed from me, and my home, and the familiar Vilna streets I love so much."[15]

Finding play under these circumstances and conditions seems somewhat startling. After all, the odds for mere survival were stacked against the children. It can be argued that, in light of the overwhelming odds, it was a miracle how many of them survived for as long as they did—and that some, as we will see, even played, though for preciously few moments. Their brief respite is not indicative of a lack of German resolve or diligence. From historical evidence it becomes apparent that the Germans simply failed to estimate the will and rationale of survival among those assigned to die. The children's unexpected vitality, ingenuity, and fight for life surprised even their executioners.

Children grew up prematurely—at least mentally—in the Holocaust, but psychological regression to almost infantile behavior also became a common phenomenon. Their physical growth was definitely retarded by hunger and a multitude of illnesses associated with ghetto living. Suffering and pain stamped their mark upon the children's bodies and psyche. They lived, and died, with the full knowledge that their actions had ramifications for those surrounding them. While hiding with her family in a small room of a farmer's house in the hills of Tuscany, a five-year-old girl, upon being suddenly discovered by a stranger, had a sense of "wanting to fall through the floor and disappear, I wanted to just melt away into nothing." After running up to the family's hiding place she was in an "absolute state of panic, because I realized that my being there could have given all of us away and that would have meant the end for all of us." She knew that discovery "meant terrible. It meant . . . it meant the worst of anything. . . . I knew it was a terrible thing."[16]

Children learned when and where to hide and how to protect their parents. When offered a sedative in a hideout, a small child of two would say "I'm not going to cry. I know the Gestapo is upstairs." Ever-lurking death instilled a powerful energy for remaining alive and grasping every opportunity to look to the future. Rudashevski, the young boy from Vilna who has been quoted earlier, formulated his view of life with these words: "I decided. I shall live with tomorrow, not with today. And if for 100 ghetto children of my age 10 can study, I must be among the fortunate ones. . . . Studying has become even more precious to me than before." The tenacious will to survive and to face the future with hope became the goal of many youngsters. Among themselves, especially in orphanages, "they expressed touching solidarity, sharing their food and helping their sick friends in difficult circumstances." They realized that although there were no mystical substitutes for food and warm clothing and sunshine, it was still possible to oppose the invading sense of futility and despair with moral resources.[17]

There were a number of ways to evade the raiding parties hunting for children. With the knowledge that working status could provide reprieve from death, it was not uncommon of children of eight and nine to volunteer for labor companies and ghetto workshops. Ghetto statistics in Lodz showed, for example, that 13,881 youngsters under seventeen were employed in the summer of 1943. Either because the father was deported to a labor camp or because the adults became demoralized by the psychological and material pressures, circumstances forced the young to assume leadership roles in many families. It was a natural process. When family members of two generations were allowed to stay together the children often acquired a greater agility in negotiating the novel demands of ghetto than their parents whose constant humiliation destroyed both their self-esteem and their will to resist. The physical and mental deterioration of a parent often made the adult dependent on the child, and the child's survival was frequently linked to his or her ability to gain authority for independent actions. There were many families in which young children, some even less than ten years old, supported, with imagination and skill, the entire group. As smugglers, the young soon became an important lifeline between the ghetto and the outside world—"the breadwinners." Songs and poems eulogized their heroism:

> Over the wall, through holes, and past the guard,
> Through the wires, ruins and fences,
> Plucky, hungry, and determined,
> I sneak through, dart like a cat.[18]

THE GERMANS MISCALCULATED, also, the reaction of society at large. With all the documents at our disposal, it seems unfair even to insinuate that the Jewish community had the power to alter the course of events. But it is undeniable, nonetheless, that the Nazi extermination plans, and the process itself, caught the Jewish community completely unprepared. The immediate consequences upon the children, and upon many adults as well, were catastrophic, as one political leader's comment reveals: "These had once been our future, these broken little bodies, these cracked voices begging for bread."[19] Following the initial shock, however, the instinctive reaction within the beleaguered Jewish communities everywhere was uniform in retooling existing institutions and creating new ones for expanded or new tasks. Among the many priorities facing them, the rescue, shelter, and protection of the young took precedence. In France, Italy, and other countries where a relatively supportive population lent a hand in rescuing children, hunger and famine were never acute problems. There, the finding of immediate shelter for the young occupied the minds of Jewish institutions. Conversely, in the ghettos and camps of the East the first order of action was to save the youth from imminent mass starvation and rampaging diseases. One could see a growing spirit of cooperation, slowly evolving as a consequence of the ongoing drama, take hold of the ghettos. It seems that neither official Jewish leadership, nor voluntary organizations and political parties, nor the masses ever came as close to unity on any given issue or policy matter as they did in the case of the perscuted children. No divisions of class, religion, or ideology existed when the children were concerned.

Tragically, it took precious time to recover from the initial shock and trauma, and during that period tens of thousands of children fell victim to hunger, disease, or Kinderaktion. But when the numbness wore off, Jewish communities everywhere geared themselves, to the extent that conditions permitted, for the rescue work. The recognition of the urgency was punctuated by scenes of unspeakable horrors. In rags, swollen from hunger, and ravaged by disease, children were evident on every street and in every ghetto by the spring of 1940. Several months later the picture of children on

Grzybowska Street in Warsaw, described by Mary Berg, herself only sixteen years old, turned more frightful:

> There are a great number of almost naked children, whose parents have died, and who sit in rags on the streets. Their bodies are horribly emaciated; one can see their bones through their parchment-like yellow skin. This is the first stage of scurvy; in the last stage of this terrible disease, the same little bodies are blown up and covered with festering wounds. Some of these children have lost their toes; they toss around and groan. They no longer have a human appearance and are more like monkeys than children. They no longer beg for bread, but for death.[20]

The sheer size of the population of the Warsaw ghetto, a half-million Jews with over one hundred thousand children under fifteen living in a most precarious position, posed unique problems for the Jewish Council there. At least three-quarters of these children needed some form of welfare assistance. Conditions prevailing in other ghettos were perhaps not much better, but solutions differed due to local conditions and the quality of leadership. The activities of Jewish councils in occupied Europe are considered one of the most controversial chapters of Jewish history. Filtered through a haze of political rivalries and the memory of anger, the genuine dismay and indignation that these councils elicited have been noted by contemporaries and historians alike. Yet if we consider their limited resources, these ignominious institutions showed a sincere concern and tenderness toward the little "urchins" of the ghetto. Even such notorious figures as Chaim Rumkowski, who was head of the Lodz Judenrat (*Aeltester der Juden* [Eldest of the Jews]) and was generally "despised and hated by every inhabitant of the ghetto," made genuine efforts to ameliorate the lot of orphaned children in the Lodz ghetto.[21]

Adam Czerniakow from the Warsaw Judenrat, who was labeled by Kaplan as a "nincompoop among nincompoops," came to the aid of the orphans in similar circumstances. He had realized the urgency of maintaining welfare among the youth as early as the summer of 1940. Less than a year into the Nazi occupation, at that point the ghetto was not yet cordoned off from the outside world, but unmistakable signs of spiritual and physical deterioration were everywhere. A May 9, 1940, entry in the journal of Emmanuel Ringelblum betrayed the terror and desperation of the Jewish child: 'I want to rob. I want to eat. I want to be a German.' " In his hunger he hated being Jewish. Several months later, Czerniakow, with the cooperation of welfare organizations, bravely moved forward with a concerted drive to collect funds for the children: the idea of the "Children's Month" was born. It was not a mere coincidence that his campaign coincided with the ban on Jews visiting city parks and playgrounds. Kaplan, who was as keeneyed as he was sharp tongued remarked on the "children's month" project that "the philanthropic noise is deafening . . . the general impression: a country fair!" Yet people gave, especially the masses: "The collectors passed over one resident named Goldman, because he was known to be impoverished. And this simple Jew was very hurt. . . . 'How can it be,' he said, 'that I have the chance to do a good deed and am not allowed to? . . . And the committee was forced to accept his donation—two days of work a month."[22] A year later, in November 1941, the same campaign was repeated but with more publicity and fanfare. "Children's Month" was declared from every wall and billboard with posters spreading slogans like "Our Children Must Not Die" or "Children Are Sacred." A sequel to this project was being planned for August 1942, but the mass deportations commencing in July of that year effectively destroyed it.

In other ghettos with autocratic leaders, the central administrations became, with varying success, the major organs for child welfare. Although no other ghetto was in any way nearly as large as the one in Warsaw, each had its own unique problems. Some of them became so inundated with refugees that they could not muster the necessary financial resources to alleviate, measurably, the plight of the young. In Lublin, for example, the number of children fed rose from 258 to over 2,000 within several months. In Vilna, and to some extent in Lodz, ghetto administrations had to grapple with the rising number of orphans following waves of executions in their vicinity. In a report, Chaim Rumkowski of Lodz listed five orphanages and an infant home in addition to kindergartens for children whose parents were both employed.[23]

An entire community came together to save at least its remnants, but it became painfully clear that the fight for the child was an uphill battle. A spoon of soup or a piece of bread could not arrest a malady which was stronger than the Judenrat. Indeed, the meals provided by public kitchens, it was admitted, did not offer enough nutrition to sustain life. "Relief only lengthens the period of suffering," a chronicler remarked, "people [children] who are fed in the public kitchens are all dying out." In spite of all the sacrifices, hunger remained the ultimate ruler of the ghetto, taking its toll incessantly among the youth. There is a degree of heroism, however, in the quiet dignity with which the children of ghettos faced death. At the funeral of young hunger victims, a participant recorded, the children of an orphanage sent a wreath inscribed: "From children who are starving to children who have died of starvation."[24]

THE DESPERATE CAMPAIGN to save the children was waged on many fronts. Indeed, the day-to-day job of staying alive required all the ingenuity and energy a community could muster. Among the wide spectrum of responses to the children's plight, particular attention was directed to play and recreational activities. In light of the dire straits under which these institutions had to function and the immediate physical peril threatening the young, this fact may seem somewhat unexpected and even disconcerting. The gnawing question as to the utility of play amidst physical and mental terror returns again and again. However, we can assume that after the physical rescue of children, protecting their spiritual, emotional, and moral universe also took on special significance. In a world of confusion, sudden change, and constant terror, the reinstatement of a precarious mental balance was almost as important as a physical equilibrium. Neither could function properly without the other.

In comparison with concentration camps, ghettos (and some transit camps) at least retained some measures of self-governemnt, which permitted a wider range of action than in the camps. The ghettos had been allocated, with deliberate malice, the most dilapidated sections of any city, places that were physically and aesthetically inhospitable and forbidding. The recognition that play might be a sheltering mechanism from this surrounding bleakness was reflected in the decision of Adam Czerniakow to launch a drive for the creation of playgrounds in the Warsaw ghetto. Unfortunately this movement happened only a few weeks before the commencement of the destruction of the Warsaw ghetto in the spring of 1942. We must marvel, just as his contemporaries did, at his resolve in concentrating his concerns and energies around playgrounds, in light of the fiscal, political, and psychological powerlessness of the Judenrat.

Czerniakow was either a brave man or, perhaps, a desperate one—the dividing line is often blurred. Nevertheless, his step indicates the importance the community attached to play as a psychological weapon in raising the morale of the adults and drawing a protective curtain around the children. Indeed, everyone needed a brief psychological respite, from which, reemerged, they could face their world. The idea created, perhaps, a world of dreams (not an escape) through which the youth could cope and understand the real world. In the words of Yitshok Rudashevski, the young ghetto boy from Vilna whose observations have been quoted: "I run through the cold sad little ghetto street . . . to fall asleep as soon as possible, because in sleep you dream and have sweeter hopes than when awake."[25]

3
Play and the Community

"Balm for the wounds.
The street is smiling!"

TO AN UNPREPARED visitor the ghettos and labor camps of Nazi Europe must have been a staggering sight—a dark forbidding landscape void of flowers and even birds. They presented a noisy, confusing mass of humanity, a place of unspeakable horror and misery, where the ubiquity of death was in fact the most ordinary feature. "I look around and find myself immersed in a terrific hum of traffic," wrote an observer from Warsaw,

> a constant rushing, pushing, moaning, crying, bickering. . . . Most strikingly, there is a dreadful population density which has no parallel in Europe. The deadly overcrowding is particularly noticeable in the streets, where people literally rub against each other, unable to cross from one sidewalk to the other without endless obstruction.[1]

The actors in this eerie landscape of human masses were the little children who "with bare feet, bare knees, and torn clothing, stand dumbly in the street weeping." To complete this picture there were the old, decrepit houses, ruins from the ravages of war, dust, smoke, and the pungent odor of burning garbage. The ghettos sprawled through the oldest and most deteriorated sections, districts, in the words of an eyewitness, "that had been an eyesore for years." From the German viewpoint, this was an ideal arrangement. It promoted an abnormally high mortality rate, and having the ghetto residents die was the main objective. It was also part of a psychological warfare, which aimed to humiliate and spiritually subjugate the population. A native writer's comments provide us with a fairly accurate picture. He has described Lodz as "the most offensively ugly" of all Polish cities, and its

3. "The Fecalists." Children pulling the refuse wagon in the Lodz ghetto, 1941–42. From the Archives of the Simon Wiesenthal Center, Los Angeles, Calif.

ghetto, located in the Balut district, was in the most gruesome condition. Unsuited for such high population density, all sanitary facilities broke down, and children pulled wagons overflowing with human excrement through the congested streets. Mountains of refuse burned in courtyards and on empty, bombed-out sites. A German officer observed that "an indescribable odor" lay over the ghetto, distinguishing it from all the surrounding areas. Other ghettos struggled with similar conditions. It was an unhealthy environment; the crowding created fertile breeding grounds for diseases and was an endless source of physical and mental torment.[2]

A ghetto was a world unto itself. Enclosed with its misery and pain, outsiders looked in with awe and disbelief. Stanislaw Rozycki, a ghetto diarist, recorded that people on the "Aryan" side "gape curiously at the piteous spectacle presented by these tattered gangs [of children]." Nothing could ameliorate the dreary landscape for there were no trees or grass. Rozycki searching for parks, gardens, or flowers in the Warsaw ghetto had to admit that "such things do not exist here. Even my yearning for modest traces of green is in vain—all this has been eliminated through cunning measures." Warsaw was especially notorious for its bareness, but other places were no better. While he could distinguish the gentle meadows and sloping hills in

4. "Jews are forbidden to enter the park." In Amsterdam, the sign's message is reinforced by grinning Aryans (1942). Courtesy of the Ghetto Fighters' Museum, Israel.

the distance, the words of a young boy in Theresienstadt betray the same quiet resignation to a world void of beauty where "butterflies don't live." Only one tree grew in the Vilna ghetto. A popular song sentimentalized:

> For them the parks and boulevards
> For me a place of misery.[3]

It has already been mentioned, and we will have occasion to mention it again, that even before the complete ghettoization, military governors and civilian representatives initiated throughout Nazi-occupied Europe a flurry of decrees placing all parks, playgrounds, swimming pools, and other recreational and cultural institutions off limits for the Jewish community. These edicts were part of deliberate policies of psychological humiliation and physical repression. An entry in Chaim Kaplan's diary on July 29, 1940, before the complete sealing off of the ghetto, recorded that SA Brigadier General Leist, the military administator of Warsaw, "has issued an order forbidding the Jews to enter the city parks or the municipal promenades." These measures reinforced the adults' demoralization and sense of helplessness and presented immense physical and psychological traumas for the children. It is little wonder that Kaplan was still confounded, two months later, by the repercussions of this decree:

> Anywhere that a tree has been planted, or a bench has been placed, Jewish children are forbidden to derive enjoyment. It pains the heart to see the sorrow of our children. Children who have never known what it is to sin are forced by order of the cruel conquerors to stay outside while children their age are romping in a half-empty park.[4]

The question of what to do about public gardens located in the Jewish quarters was also an issue, and in some places it occupied the attention of Jewish institutions. Plans had to be submitted to the SS administrations who erased any hope that might have remained: the parks in question were either closed off or excised from the ghettos. Before full ghettoization, these policies also encompassed popular children's institutions which were basically Jewish to begin with: Maccabi sports clubs, boy scout organizations, and other groups were banned. For Jewish children there would be no more clubs, societies, sports teams, visits to museums or zoological gardens, attendance at sports events. At the first stage of the occupation, all purely Jewish associations were disbanded altogether. A stern official warning was issued, as in Holland: "Many a Jew will lose his life for taking an over-lax view of this decree." A few years later, in 1943, the collaborating French government followed suit and enacted similar legislation for the dissolution of the Jewish Scout movement.[5]

These decrees took a very human toll in tears and pain. To write about them now is to state history, but to be fourteen and encounter their effect in the summer of 1941, as Éva Székely did in the middle of the start of the 400-meter breaststroke, must have been a fundamental shock. She was called back from the block, just as the race was starting. She lived to win the gold medal in the London Olympiad of 1948, but at that moment in Budapest she experienced only great hurt. This talented swimmer was only one among millions of children throughout Europe who were forced to tortuously adjust the economies of their souls to humiliation.[6]

These exclusionary measures in the newly conquered territories followed a rather predictable pattern that had been started in Germany itself, and then later in Austria. Jews were segregated and not allowed to use the parks, playgrounds, or similar establishments altogether after 1938. Still, this decree in Warsaw was alarming enough to propel Adam Czerniakow to convey a protest in his weekly report to the authorities "against the prohibition of the use of parks." In spite of his cautiously formulated words, a stern reprimand from the Nazi administration quickly reestablished the fact that no precarious dialogue could be conducted between the conquerors and the vanquished. "You allow yourself to criticize the orders of SA Brigadier General Leist," a memo warned Czerniakow. "May I call to your attention that any repetition of such conduct will be answered with severest measures."[7]

This controversial man will be quoted often in this book, and some fleshing out seems called for. After assuming the leadership of the Jewish community of Warsaw in 1939, Czerniakow presided over a half million people. He is often depicted as incompetent and ineffectual, but in reality he exemplified both Jewish helplessness in the face of the mightiest death machine Western civilization has ever known and, in his representation of the ghetto, Jewish dignity and honor. In his contacts with the Nazi administration he argued repeatedly that if the city parks were forbidden to the Jews, the ghetto should be allowed a park of its own. His negotiations with the authorities about the inclusion of Krasinski Park, like other dealings he had with the Germans, can be characterized as a roller coaster of hope and despair. He would alternately receive reassurances and outright rejections. Based on several entries in his diaries it seems certain that he is not at fault for the final decree excluding the park from the ghetto. His efforts show his deep concern about the loss of greenery and the lack of opportunities for exercise and fresh air for the youngsters, concern that reflected the prevailing attitudes within the entire community, which had become justifiably alarmed about the demoralizing atmosphere, the unhealthy conditions, and the absence of an outlet for the creative energy of the children.[8]

Similar apprehensions were expressed in other locales as well. In 1942 the official chronicle of the Lodz ghetto took special notice of the sad lot of children behind the "walls":

> Just beyond the outer limit of the ghetto, on Urzednicza Street at the barbed-wire fence, an amusement park has been set up, as it was last year. The main attraction, the only one visible, is a suspension-type merry-go-around. Every day the children of the ghetto make a pilgrimage to this corner and gaze longingly at the activities on the other side of the fence. It is mostly children too on the other side, who are romping about and climbing into the small hanging boats of the merry-go-around. A radio amplifier broadcasts phonograph music. The ghetto children have never seen a carousel and have seldom heard music. They listen and peer at a curious, alien world, where children live in a sort of never-never land. A merry-go-round, almost within reach, only the barbed wire keeps them away. Children are children on either side of the barbed wire—and yet they are not the same.[9]

EVEN A CURSORY examination would show ghettos and camps to be physically debilitating and morally depressing places. The adjustments that adults made to their new surroundings were painfully difficult, but their successes in escaping the depravity depended, to a great extent, on resources they had within themselves. The children, on the other hand, had to rely on the abilities and resources of the adults for the creation of any semblance of an environment, like the world left on the other side of the barbed wire. The available options and means of the adults were greatly limited, which was only a reflection of their general powerlessness. Despite the imposed restraints, one of the rare areas of action was the building of parks, playgrounds, clubs, and other play opportunities. These projects, however, were always undertaken during the periodic lulls in Nazi terror, which also corresponded with some stabilization in ghetto life. In a rare confluence of opinions, the community (parents, educators, political activists, and community leaders) realized that play could furnish a thin veneer of protection from the negative effects of ghetto existence.

Health posed the most immediate and eminent concern for parents who were the first to understand and appreciate the life-preserving importance of parks and gardens in providing the children with fresh air, exercise, and play. A mother, one of the very few who had a choice in the matter, refused to put her son in school in the Theresienstadt camp. "I had my choice for Josef—school or work on the farm," she rationalized later. "I chose the farm. He would have fresh air, exercise, more food. There would be plenty of time to educate him, if we lived to be liberated."[10] This example was, of course, an exception rather than the rule. In other ghettos very few alternatives were left to many of the parents.

In Warsaw and in other Eastern European ghettos, conditions were much worse, both materially and environmentally. During the early stages of ghettoization, at least until the full enclosure of the ghetto (c. 1939–40), mothers were willing to face serious retribution for taking their children, surreptitiously, to the forbidden paradise of the city parks. Their determination is admirable; by slipping through the ghetto gates and taking off their arm-bands, mothers put themselves and their children at risk of immediate arrest. It was a nerve-racking experience because, even if they could temporarily hide their identity, the ruse provided them with no psychological reassurance. Janina David recalls her outings as a little girl to the Warsaw city parks during the spring or summer of 1940: "Mother insisted on going to the park. We needed fresh air, and we were going to get it. . . . In the parks Mother encouraged me to play with the children, but I was shy. Instinctively I knew that we had nothing in common any more."[11] Several months later, the hermetic sealing off of the Warsaw ghetto brought to a halt these forbidden excursions to the city parks.

Although some parents, especially the well educated and wealthy, equated fresh air open spaces, and exercise with health and, consequently, survival, only a minority actually left the ghetto clandestinely to achieve those benefits. The lower classes possessed neither the consciousness nor the physical tenacity to sneak out to the green parks. When finding daily bread became a grueling struggle, visits to parks were seldom a priority, and in the face of their complete segregation from the surrounding communities, ghetto dwellers were forced to adjust to the limitations of their pitiful universe. The majority of children never left the ghetto and fast became accustomed to its bleak existence. Rachel Auerbach, whose impressions from the Warsaw ghetto often included moments from the everyday lives of the inhabitants, wrote that a mother, "who happened to see a few sprigs of lilac on our kitchen table, begged to borrow only one sprig—just to show it to her little child who had never seen a lilac, or even a flower, in his short life."[12]

The ability of children and parents to adjust to the abnormal situations that the Holocaust provided is one of the marvels of the human psyche and a powerful testimony to a tenacious need to normalize disrupted lives. The ever-observant Kaplan noticed in Warsaw that "Jewish mothers have already gotten used to their bad fortune and in order not to deprive their babies of the sunlight, they take their stand with their cradles wherever there is a square or a vacant lot, or side walk covered with sunlight." Mothers in Bialystok reacted in a similar fashion, making their "demonstrative strolls," as a Judenrat memo phrased it, "with their colorful baby carriages on streets visible to the outside world." This might be a mistake, an appeal from the Judenrat reasoned, because it could provoke the SS and security police into conducting a Kinderaktion.[13]

In the crowded quarters where eight to ten people often lived in one room, only the cluttered, dirty courtyards and bombed-out houses were available for play places. In Warsaw no parks were located within the boundaries of the ghetto. In Bialystok there was only one small public playground for 35,000 inhabitants. Whatever small plots existed were utilized, invariably, for home gardening to ease the plight of the starving community. As an alternative, the "houses with flat roofs have been transformed into city beaches," young Mary Berg mentioned in her diary. Many tenants "either paid for the luxury to sit and sunbathe in an enclosed small space" or came to utilize the roofs, as did Berg, "where the air is pure. . . . and I think of the wide world, of distant lands, of freedom." By the summer of 1941 a lively trade sprang up in free spaces; private yards turned into rudimentary gardens by enterprising owners became precious commodities and were rented out as outdoor coffee shops for the adults and playgrounds for the young. Noticing the mushrooming gardens in the ghetto, Kaplan remarked on the new phenomenon with an element of sarcasm:

> Is there a tree in them? Not necessarily. Have they wide-open spaces and freedom? Nothing of the sort. Desolate, lonely lots, surrounded by high walls at the backs of courtyards or planted in the space between the houses of the wall have been turned into "parks." Mothers and children fill them. For space for a baby's cradle they pay 50 zloty a month, and if any member of the family besides the mother accompanies or comes to visit the child, he must pay an additional admission charge. Old people and invalids who want to relax and enjoy the "beauties of nature" pay two zloty a day. The unemployed young people play games there, and fill the garden with gaiety and lightheartedness.[14]

It required all the power of human imagination to see the new institutions as "parks" in the traditional sense of the word. They also fostered a divisiveness within the community, as Ringelblum thunders indignantly in an entry in his diary from May 1941: "Naturally, the children of the rich can enjoy them, because the charge is from 30–40 to 70 zlotys a month. The poor children never see a patch of grass. Traffic in fresh air?" Considering that workers in a ghetto shop earned less than six zlotys a day, he was correct in stating that only the affluent could send their young to these playgrounds. Yet, with all the inequities, the parks offered an alternative to parents who believed in the value of exercise and play and who could, obviously, afford it. When the authorities excluded the only park that originally belonged to the ghetto, Krasinski Park, it left a population of 150,000 children without a public playground. Janina David came from a relatively wealthy family that could afford to enroll her for three afternoons each week in a rented "park." She vividly remembered the moments she spent as a child in the expensive private playground:

> The price of admission was high. . . . But mother insisted. It was dangerous to be in the streets the whole day, the courtyard was too small and too crowded and the foul smell from the rubbish-heap was becoming unbearable. The playground was too crowded to allow any running about but there were a few trees and grass patches there, and even a few flowers managed to grow for a time. . . . There was enough space for a net-ball [volleyball] team but there was always a queue to join in the game. Mother would not allow me to take a book there to read. I was supposed to spend my time playing and getting some exercise.[15]

In Warsaw by the spring of 1941, and in other ghettos somewhat later, the schools, which were banned previously by military degrees, reopened at least partially. Operating clandestinely and under trying circumstances, these ghetto schools could capture, however, only a fraction of the youth population. The overwhelming majority of the children roamed the streets unsupervised, left to their own devices either because they were orphans or because both parents worked from dawn to dusk. The immediate task of organizing these street "urchins" and creating a livable environment for them fell to a complex mesh of self-help organizations that enveloped many ghettos; various youth movements aligned with political parties, religious bodies and, in Warsaw in particular, tenement and courtyard committees. In cooperation with welfare agencies like CENTOS (Central Shelter for Children and Orphans), YYGA (Jewish Social Self-Aid Society), ZOT (Society for the Preservation of Health), and ZTOS (Jewish Society for Social Welfare), these groups were perhaps the most pivotal grass-roots institutions of children's care and welfare. Their strength lay in their close proximity to the needs of their constituency, acting as perhaps the most important link between the official leadership and the masses. Each was a microcosm of community, involving young and old in its operations. Diarists especially praised them for planting and cultivating patches of greenery and for installing benches, deck chairs, and sandboxes in the dusty courtyards. Indeed, these courtyards fulfilled an important social role in the ghetto by becoming community centers for the inhabitants. Primarily designed for the children, and appropriately named "Children's Corners," it was to these that the young came to play, sharing with the elderly and the invalids the sun and enjoying the view of the sky, which reminded them of the "open spaces of the burgeoning world of nature outside the wall."[16]

Intended to serve as a basic welfare agency at first, the committees soon were forced to deal with every aspect of the existence of their constituents. Young people, activists in the Zionist and Bundist political movements, provided the manpower for the committees' daily tasks and special activities: operating soup kitchens, caring for children in ad hoc nurseries, organizing play activities in kindergartens, and teaching the young. Almost every courtyard had a kindergarten—"though they had, in reality, only a name to recall a happier past." Bernard Goldstein, an eminent Bund leader in Poland, drew a touching courtyard scene:

> Somewhere in the courtyard a group of children dance in a circle, clapping their hands, singing a simple melody. Their attention was concentrated completely on a girl of fourteen or fifteen who led them in their play. . . . this was a kindergarten led by a young member of our Skif.[17]

Huge tenement blocks, enclosing a courtyard on four sides, were typical to Warsaw. In Lublin, Lodz, Vilna, Cracow, and elsewhere living accommodations differed greatly from those of Warsaw, so the power of the tenement committees and their involvement in child care was never as strong in these ghettos as in the Polish capital. Alongside the Jewish Councils, which often supervised or circumscribed political activities in their locale, there was also a diverse patchwork of youth movements, ranging from the traditionalist to the Zionists and socialists (e.g. Tsukunft, Skif, Dror, Gordonia, Shomer Hatzair, and Hehalutz), which maintained the only semi-autonomous network of children's institutions. The initial motivation of these political groups, which was to protect and shelter their own party members, soon gave way to general welfare work. The stated goal of the tenement committees in Sosnowitz was similar to the rationale elsewhere: "to procure bread for the hungry." Soon, however, it became apparent that the overextended bureaucracy of the Judenrat was not able to deal with the everyday problems of the masses, and the tenement committees were forced to expand their activities into establishing and overseeing educational and play opportunities.

Among the political movements, the Bund was perhaps the most organized and disciplined group. It retained its basic infrastructure during the war, and early in the German occupation it began to function in Poland and the Baltic States. Through the efforts of some dedicated leaders, it reactivated its youth divisions, Tsukunft and Skif, and its physical education association, Morgenstern. The latter assembled children for mass and rhythmic gymnastics and sports activities; Tsukunft and Skif became responsible for the operation of summer camps for children.

The conditions under which organizational work had to be carried out were far from idyllic. During the hot summer months, day camps sprouted up in the ruins of Warsaw. Under the guidance of teachers and youth counselors children played games, sang, and danced. The camps were better than the sweltering and crowded apartments, but people burned their refuse in what open spaces were available, "enveloping the children's day camps in a foul fog from the smoldering heaps of garbage."[18] The Lodz ghetto, in spite of its unsavory reputation, was in a more advantageous position than many of the other ghettos because it contained within its boundaries a small semi-rural suburb, Marysin, where various youth groups, with the blessing of the mercurial Rumkowski, could establish summer camps and children's homes. By the end of July 1941, over fifteen hundred children were placed there. A day camp for children from four to seven years old also functioned until the fall of 1942, when the entire colony was surrounded by soldiers and its inhabitants taken to the Chelmno extermination camp. The

5. A children's playground in Marysin, Lodz ghetto, 1941–42. Courtesy of Ghetto Fighters' Museum, Israel.

police also raided the ghetto's kindergartens, orphanages, and private homes, leaving the city virtually without children under ten years old.

Operating under the nominal aegis of the Judenrat and supported by various self-help organizations, many children's institutions and boarding homes made concerted efforts, as conditions permitted, to introduce a sense of normalcy. Since food was the most precious commodity of ghetto existence, everything revolved around it. Soup kitchens evolved, by force of necessity, into youth centers augmenting nourishment with educational and recreational activities. Indeed, the Central Shelter for Children and Orphans (CENTOS) and the Society for the Preservation of Health (ZOT) were the most active and influential self-help groups directly involved in organizing children's play activities in Poland. The Warsaw center of CENTOS encompassed over one hundred institutions, catering to almost a quarter of the children (25,000) of the ghetto. Acting as departments of child and health care of the Judenrat, they financed not only the twenty soup kitchens but also close to fifty year-round day-care centers and clubs where education, culture, and recreation were offered as well as food, providing "some festiveness," as an educator termed it, "in their dreadful lives." Along with the creation of "Children's Corners," in which CENTOS was instrumental, even a permanent puppet theater was established to entertain children under its care. These and similar institutions taught art, music, dance, and supervised play as integral parts of their curriculum. Among the eight by-laws of three such institutions in Warsaw, apparently belonging to CENTOS, several clear references to this purpose can be found:

> 3. Recognizing these precarious times, we want to envelop the soul of our children with activities. . . .
> 5. We should make all efforts to provide the children with activities [that will] elicit maximum joy and happiness.

To implement the goals and objectives of the by-laws, the constitution stipulated that the educational staff should incorporate into the program an awareness of greenery, play, hygiene, and exercise:

> 5. We are to instill in the children an aesthetic appreciation of their surrounding . . . direct their attention to growing plants that might bring them closer to nature and provide them with aesthetic experiences. . . .
> 11. We are to introduce the children to all kinds of games.
> 12. Before a meal, preferably, at least 5 minutes should be devoted to exercise.
> 13. Entertainment and children's festivals should be organized on all proper occasions.[19]

Educational and play activities complimented each other in the lives of the children in child-care institutions and in the school systems as well. Formal education—and then only on the elementary level—and the reopening of the Jewish school system in Warsaw and other ghettos did not become a reality until 1941, after a sustained struggle. Although these efforts affected only a part of the youth population, the schools still faced almost insurmountable problems in ghetto circumstances. One of the major challenges facing the newly created institutions was finding suitable accommodations, not only for the educational pursuits but for play and exercise as well.

Ghetto educators became convinced of the importance of play and exercise in combating the debilitating influences of the abysmal surroundings. In this view, the mental and physical health of the children had a decisive influence on their ability to learn and develop. Similarly, play was seen as an essential part of normal growth for it "trains the powers of mind and body." These beliefs in the moral and health benefits of play and physical activity prompted close cooperation between educators and playground personnel. Orphanages and schools, especially in Warsaw, coordinated their play programs with the playgrounds and Children's Corners so that "every class could visit one."

If exercise and play were important during normal times, administrators and educators quickly came to utilize play as a re-creative and therapeutic intervention technique during times of exceptional mental and physical duress. In the Vilna ghetto, a visitor to kindergarten saw children "dancing and singing . . . [who] look well, are neatly dressed and washed. This too is one of the wonders of the ghetto." Orphanages took in perhaps the most traumatized among ghetto youth, and educators sincerely believed in play as the most effective method to reach these children. Janusz Korczak, an internationally respected educator, pediatrician, and writer, directed the most famous among the orphanages, the Dom Sierot (Orphans' Home). His inexplicable success in creating a fragile island, often threatened with destruction, amidst death is one of the enduring stories of the Holocaust. The "Old Doctor," as he affectionately was called, was a firm believer in the re-creative power of play. He tirelessly cajoled, warned, and threatened the Judenrat and individuals into supporting his wards. In one of his many appeals, he wrote in 1940: "Peaceably they run about and play, the children who came recently with wounds on their frozen fingers and toes, abused, hungry, hunted. . . . "[20]

THE OFFICIAL JEWISH leadership, i.e., the Jewish Councils, was cognizant of and willing to address the children's plight. Powerless in many respects and with needs beyond their control, the Councils nevertheless had the freedom to dispense their financial resources—as limited as they were. Originally no apparatus within the Judenrat was specifically designated to deal with child care, education, and play activities. There were a few instances when leading Jewish welfare organizations took upon themselves, with some financial backing by the Judenrat, these services. More often than not, however, these institutions, through a spontaneous process and as a consequence of the growing needs within the community, transformed themselves into semi-autonomous departments of the Judenrat. Although their jurisdiction often overlapped, as is the case in all large bureaucracies, departments of health, social welfare, education, culture, and sport were entrusted with the organization of play activities within the ghettos.

While Jewish life was severely circumscribed by official edicts before the complete physical segregation of the Jews, a certain degree of independence in cultural and recreational matters existed within the newly created ghettos and camps. Heinz Auserwald, the German kommissar of Warsaw, quite unabashedly reasoned in a memo that "the widest freedom accorded to the Jews until now [is] in so-called cultural activities. . . . All these measures have produced a certain reassurance which is necessary if their economic capacity is to be exploited for our purposes."[21] Indeed, no specific injunctions were introduced against the erection of playgrounds, planting of parks, or organizing play activities within the ghettos themselves. The building of three public playgrounds in the Warsaw ghetto commenced in the spring of 1942 and coincided with a certain degree of economic and psychological stabilization within the ghetto during temporary relaxation of German terror. It is almost impossible to reconstuct precisely the turn of events leading to Czerniakow's decision to proceed with these projects. When completed, however, they were impressive affairs. And, to believe a survivor's recollection, the playground in front of the community building was perhaps the most advanced establishment of its kind in all Warsaw.

Be that as it may, we must reiterate that without the cooperation of a large segment of ghetto society neither Czerniakow nor other community leaders could have been successful, given the severely limited resources. It was a small miracle how much was achieved in the area of youth welfare. Mary Berg graphically described, in a diary entry for May 6, 1942, one of the remarkable examples of such community spirit. The young people of her art school in the Warsaw ghetto decided to provide a more attractive environment for play.

> Yesterday Professor Greifenberg took all the students in his class at our school to the little park opposite the community building. This park is on the site of a bombed house, where the Toporol gardeners have planted grass and flowers. Today it is green there. Jewish workmen have constructed swings, benches, etc. The pupils of our school went to paint a fresco of animal cartoons on one of the walls of the ruined house.[22]

Building playgrounds and creating play opportunities for the horror-stricken youth of the ghettos was a complex undertaking. It appears that many of the leaders, middle-class and well educated, understood, scientifically and intuitively, the practical and spiritual importance of parks and green areas in the dreary lives of ghetto inhabitants. Their views were based on the belief that playgrounds and activities could offer mental and physical health, a psychological buffer, social stability, and order in face of crisis.

It is not superfluous to reiterate that ghettos, and even more so the camps, were not healthy places. "Due to undernourishment," a historian from Lodz noted, "young children learned late walking and speaking, and older ones stopped growing." Also, if one examines the extant child mortality statistics, specifically those for death from tuberculosis, the importance attached to these green areas amidst dirt and fetidity becomes readily apparent. They were to act, within the rubble-covered eyesores, as "lungs for the ghetto," purifying its air and the spirit of its young. Again, Kaplan's comment on the subject gives a fair record of the prevailing view in the community: "It is now three years since we have seen grass growing and flowers in bloom. Even before we were shoved into the ghetto we were forbidden to enter the city parks. Inside the parks there was space and breadth."[23]

The health officials of Vilna shared the opinions of their colleagues in Warsaw. In an effort to control strumosis, groups of children were ordered to spend as much time in the fresh air and sunshine as possible. In lieu of parks, for which no immediate space was available, small flower beds were planted close to the ghetto fence, "where children could play and sometimes pick a flower." With dogged determination, ghetto authorities succeeded in convincing the Nazi officers to allow children's excursions to the neighboring woods. These hikes were supervised by medical staff and teachers.

The psychological well-being of the children and the adults was also a major concern of the Jewish administrations. Thus, another weighty rationale for the creation of playgrounds was "to give the ghetto children a sense of freedom," as a young observer phrased it. The playground was intended to become a tiny oasis of peace and the games were to provide the children with rare moments of joy, erecting symbolic walls against the harshness and ugliness of reality. The commanding impulse behind it was linked to the will of the masses to live and survive by any means—"Tzu iberleybn" [santification of life], in Yiddish. This spirit promoted the belief that a people who were able to laugh and create in such terrible circumstances would be able to outlive its oppressors. In the words of Kaplan, who did not live to see the liberation, "A nation that can live in such terrible circumstances as these without losing its mind, without committing suicide—and which can still laugh—is sure of survival."[24]

Children's play constituted a part of this quest for survival. Civic leaders as well as educators hoped that play would surround the children with a protective cloak—a spiritual shelter from which the wounds of the ghetto would not seem as horrifying. That this notion was a highly romantic, almost mythical, belief in the power of play is almost incidental. The importance of myths is not that they are true or false, but that they are somehow there when people need them. With all its positive influences, play had very little potential to mold or alter life. In fact, the protective walls erected against reality were, as will be shown, fragile creations that could provide only a few moments of genuine joy and a fleeting respite from a depressing surrounding.

Jewish community leaders clung to these beliefs in the importance of play with a desperation that could come only from a sense of powerlessness in dealing with the problems of the youth. As the head of the Lodz Judenrat and a former administrator of an orphanage himself, Chaim Rumkowski seemed to evince true affection for the children of the Lodz ghetto. He personally inspected a series of sites for a permanent playground in the spring of 1941 because the old one was taken over for vegetable gardens. It was to accommodate over a thousand children and was planned to include a host of activities. For its opening a special appeal to the children was disseminated by the department of education on May 4, 1941:

> Children! In order to provide the feeble and weakened inmates of the ghetto with some relaxation, the enjoyment of a little fresh air, and to improve the appearance of the ghetto in general, we are building a park with open grassy plazas and squares, and benches for all. These plazas and squares must be protected from vandalism, do not damage the benches, do not step on the grass and planted places nor pull out the trees and break the branches. That would be, of course, very unfair [unfortunate] toward your brothers and sisters. It would sadden, also, our good tradesman who installed them, as well as Mr. Rumkowski, the Chairman.[25]

Rumkowski left no literary legacy and his actions reverberate, for the most part negatively, through the voices and judgments of others. Czerniakow, on the other hand, recorded his innermost thoughts on many subjects in the pages of his diary. An emotionally charged note by him reveals his anguish over the plight of the young. During the opening of a playground in 1942, when perhaps 50,000 children had already perished, he met with representatives of the gangs roaming the ghetto: "They are living skeletons from the ranks of the street beggars. . . . They talked with me like grown-ups—those eight-year-old citizens. I am ashamed to admit it, but I wept as I have not wept for a long time."[26]

It is not difficult to understand the impulses that propelled Czerniakow to build the playgrounds. His love of children is obvious. A tautly voiced entry also reveals that he felt deep compassion toward the mothers who sat with their babies "among the ruins of the bombed-out hospital." At the end, Warsaw boasted three park-playground complexes: on Grzybowska, Nalewki, and Nowolipki streets. Czerniakow considered these to be one of the crowning achievements of his administration and made every effort to open them with appropriate ceremony. At the openings, in the presence of high-ranking Nazi officials, invited educators, and parents, entertainment was provided by the Jewish Police orchestra, choirs, dance groups, and gymnasts, after which molasses candy was given to the children.

The recreation programs were coordinated with the teaching schedules of the schools and day-care centers so that every class could visit the playgrounds twice a week. "For a few short hours," a survivor recalled, "the lit-

6. Chaim Rumkowski and his wife review a children's parade in Marysin, Lodz ghetto, 1940–41. From the Archives of the Simon Wiesenthal Center, Los Angeles, Calif.

tle ones could forget the fears which they felt no less than their elders, and be children again." Janusz Korczak's wards often visited these parks, marching in an orderly fashion with the "Old Doctor" bringing up the rear. The playground supervisors and counselors received the children with smiles and laughs. "Laugh! Laugh!" a supervisor encouraged her helpers. "We have to bathe our children in laughter."[27]

While ghetto councils faced grave difficulties in creating a livable environment, however tenuous, for the children, it was an even greater wonder that Auschwitz, Bergen Belsen, and other camps (among them Theresienstadt and Westerbrok are especially noteworthy) possessed some rudimentary system of child care. As camps, Westerbork and Theresienstadt occupied a paradoxical yet unique position in the Nazi camp universe. Although neither possessed extermination facilities, both exhibited, to a large degree, many of the horrors and cruelties of concentration camps. Westerbork, under the command of Obersturmfuehrer Albert Gemmeker, a rather capricious and sometimes even humane SS officer, served as a transit camp for Dutch Jewry en route to Auschwitz and Bergen Belsen. An old fortress town in Bohemia, Theresienstadt was the brain child of Reinhard Heydrich, who wanted to present the world with a showcase ghetto (*Mustergetto*). In reality, however, for German, Czech, and Danish Jews its function was similar to that of Westerbork. Both camps enjoyed a limited self-government, which, in turn, permitted an extensive youth-welfare program. Given the sparse financial resources, lack of food, and the constant dread of transports (from there they went to Auschwitz), the adults in both camps succeeded in creating a genuine oasis for the youth. It is also likely that the occupation authorities themselves condoned play activities, although there was little altruism in their thinking. They assumed that such outlets might have a calming effect upon the agitated population. Philip Mechanicus, a sharp-eyed observed at Westerbork, sarcastically noted:

> Commandant [Gemmeker] has said that he thinks Jews who work all day long need relaxation. . . . The Obersturmfuehrer is such a good psychologist that he knows this law of life and has put it into effect here? Or is he merely a brutal egoist who lets the Jews amuse themselves for his own amusement and gives them something at the same time?"

Introspective and modest, known by his beret and pipe, Mechanicus was a trained journalist, a European man of letters; he perished in Auschwitz. His diary outlines the bizarre social-cultural milieu of Westerbork; the sporadic interest in concerts, parties, revue, sports, and play activities, and the final bewildering realization that "Westerbork was another word for purgatory." He wrote in 1943:

> The playground is ready: four seesaws, two horizontal bars and a sandpit. I now feel as if I am living in a rather primitive little hotel somewhere out in the wilds where they have made an effort to lay something on for the children too. Guards look out from their tower all day long at the sandpit and the children playing. Later on one of them is bound to write a book called: "The Jewish Children in the Sandpit and Me."[28]

It might be of interest to interject another example of German "generosity" toward children's play. The commandant of the Riga ghetto, Karl Wilhelm Krause who was known to personally shoot inmates, held strikingly generous views about child care. His was one of the schizophrenic minds so characteristic of the SS hierarchy. An example of his perversity can be seen in his permitting the construction of a rudimentary playground in close proximity of the gallows. After executions, the commandant was often seen to go to the sandbox and give chocolates and candy to the playing children; he liked to be called "Uncle Krause." He ordered a former dance instructor to give gymnastic and ballet lessons to the young inmates. Perhaps it never

7. Youth dancing in the Westerbork camp, 1942–43. Courtesy of Rijksinstituut voor Oorlogsdocumentatie.

seemed incongruous to the benevolent commandant that he ordered periodic sweeps of the ghetto and sent the same children to extermination camps.[29]

As long as play was not interfering with discipline or work, the SS commandants of Theresienstadt, three in succession, also tolerated the recreational pursuits of the young. Many of the surviving children's paintings betray their creators' preoccupation with the rare moment of joy that play could provide. Administered by the Jugendfuersorge (Youth Care Service), morning exercises, daily play sessions, and competitive games served as integral parts of the educational process. Beyond that, youth sports and games were designed to improve health as well as morale. For their part, the children immersed themselves in these pastimes with a fury and desperation that must have been fueled by a clear knowledge of temporality governing a fragile presence. The games themselves created an animated atmosphere not only for the youth but also for the adults. Attending these games gave the older generation, whose sharply defined world adjusted to the deadly schedule of the deportation trains, an opportunity to escape from a reality over which they had no control.

In some ways Theresienstadt was an anomaly within the Nazi ghetto system. The children received, at least in the Children's Homes, better food and housing conditions than adults. The overwhelming majority of them lived in collectives (homes) under the care of a highly dedicated staff. These and a few other factors ensured that they did not succumb to the demoralization that was evident in other ghettos and camps. Every home had its team, its banner, and its uniform. The topic of conversation invariably revolved around the games of the day. H. G. Adler, a sociologist and an inmate of the camp, explained: "no individual could tear himself away from the camp activities, other than by death. And no one could escape participating in the activities too long for the camp was a powerful institution of participation."[30]

One cannot fail to mention, however, briefly, also the tragic figure of Freddy Hirsch, a German Maccabi sport instructor, who was the moving force behind youth activities in Theresienstadt. Later, when he and several thousand inmates were deported to the Auschwitz/Birkenau extermination complex, he succeeded in creating a small oasis for the children even in that inferno. As the "Head of the Children's Day Block" in the so-called Family Camp, he was responsible for building a playground and organizing recreational activities. The Family Camp was one of the most diabolical inventions of the Nazi mind. The brain child of Adolf Eichmann, it came into existence in the fall of 1943 and housed 4,000 Czech Jews deported from Theresienstadt. With the aim of distracting attention from the "death factory" and not arousing panic, the deportees were at first well treated by the guards and allowed to establish an elaborate educational and recreational program. To complete the deception, an artist-inmate was commissioned to decorate "the children's barracks to their [German] specifications with Disney's Snow White and the Seven Dwarfs in giant size on the inner walls." The sight of children playing freely, unhindered and apparently not on their way to the crematorium, was the source of amazement for the regular prisoners in the camp—it was unheard of in the history of Auschwitz. "I watched in wonder across the wire as they organized their new and temporary lives . . . " Rudolf Vrba, a veteran Auschwitz inmate recalled. "I saw them set aside a barrack for the children, a nursery, no less, in the shadow of the crematorium. I saw a blond, athletic man of about thirty [Freddy Hirsch] organizing games, then lessons."[31] In reality, however, there was no escape from Auschwitz. Six months later, while Freddy Hirsch poisoned himself, the entire Family Camp was sent to the gas chambers.

The Family Camp was not the only facility in the Auschwitz/Birkenau complex where some youngsters, especially after 1944, were permitted to stay—if only briefly. In the fall of 1944, for example, twenty young children between six and twelve years of age were placed in Barrack 11 of Block B1 in the Birkenau camp for the purpose of tuberculosis experiments and other pseudo-scientific studies. It was remarkable that these children, and several dozen twins under the supervision of the infamous Dr. Mengele, were allowed to live. The barracks were heated and the meals were almost sufficient. Polish nurses, entrusted with their care, sheltered them with motherly tenderness—remembering, perhaps, their own children who had left long before toward the chimneys belching black smoke. The nurses recalled little rhymes and games, using them as one of the few remaining means in their power to bring a smile to the thin faces of the young inmates. They sang songs, comforted them in their loneliness, and taught them games.

The trail of suffering of these twenty children did not end in Birkenau. This kingdom of death, and its whirlwind of terror, had an awesome power over its victims. Transferred to the Neuengamme concentration camp near Hamburg, the children were subjected to painful medical experiments, worthless as they turned out, after which the majority of them became seriously ill. Their pain and tragic fate have been described in vivid colors by Gunther Schwarberg in his book *The Murders at Bullenhuser Dam*. The struggle of the adult prisoners to keep the children alive and to brighten their final hours is one of the lesser known sagas of the era. A whole camp was moved to tears for the children who were strangers to them. Even some SS men were touched by their sufferings. Amidst the surrealistic landscape of human misery, the camp inmates retained their humanity by showing compassion and solidarity with the suffering children. While utterly powerless and in need themselves, they gave secret sweets and homemade wooden toys—horses, cars, a wagon, a doll in a cradle—to the little prisoners. The children went to their inevitable death with their crude toys in their hands—the SS men hanged them, as one prisoner observed, "like pictures hung up on a wall on hooks."[32]

A brief comment should also be made about the transit and collection camps in France that came into existence following the capitulation of that country to the Nazis. At first these centers held foreign-born Jews who were incarcerated by French police under German pressure. Relief programs for the children in such notorious camps as Gurs, Rivesaltes, and Drancy had their origins in French law, which did not oppose humanitarian aid. A Swiss volunteer in Camp des Mills described that camp as a dreary and forlorn place. There was a general "absence of movement, the suppression of daily walks for the adults, lack of playgrounds for the children." "Roving teams" of social workers—representatives of French-Jewish groups, volunteers from neutral countries, and the Society of Friends—moved in to alleviate the children's suffering: nursery schools, kindergartens, and playgrounds were hastily organized, and even caloric intake was increased. These measures were part of the efforts to make life easier, though they could not provide the most precious commodity, a lease on life.[33]

IN EXAMINING THE objectives and rationale of children's play it seems obvious that, although the adults viewed the activities with a large degree of idealism, they seemed to offer definite practical advantages as well. On the face of it, the building of playgrounds was absurd, almost delusional, particularly at a time when thousands had already perished. However, playgrounds, just like some cultural activities, became a part of the campaign to preserve a community that had once been a healthy living organism but had been humiliated morally and decimated physically. Bernard Goldstein's words provide revealing clues about the prevailing atmosphere; "to defend ourselves against the feeling of helplessness that engulfed us," he wrote after the war, "we tried to rebuild and strengthen all the prewar institutions, to create at least the illusion of a life that used to be."[34]

Though it could not provide total insulation from the surrounding reality—and perhaps was not intended to—the sight of playing children was a tonic for the persecuted population. As a form of a psychological defense mechanism, it was more than just escape from reality. Indeed, the efforts to provide play opportunities and environments were among the rare instances when the community could actively pursue initiatives in molding a reality for itself—limited as the pursuit might be. Behind the softness and innocence of children's play lay the day-to-day struggle, fortitude, and intelligence of the many individuals working out their own somewhat more bearable world.

Children's play had the power not only to ease but also to actually promote mental adaptation of the adult population to the novel demands of ghetto existence. Providing opportunities for play was part of a conscious escape mechanism through which the adult population attempted to transcend in spirit both the physical walls of the ghetto and the mental walls of terror. A curious radiance descended on the tormented faces of parents viewing their children play, recite poems, or sing. In Warsaw, several young girls formed an acrobatic group and put "on a reckless performance" as the parents "gasped" in looking at them. Other parents saw during the Lag Ba'omer festival of May 1942—Day of the Child declared by Czerniakow—how the faces of hundreds of children, clean and radiant, ignited hope in the hearts of the parents "that these innocent little creatures will awake to a better tomorrow. . . . " A hope in the future is perhaps one of the most sustaining of sentiments—especially when the present is so dismal. A ghetto official from Vilna expressed similar emotions:

> fathers and mothers, who had to work from dusk to dawn, were the most devoted participants of children's festivals and holidays, eliciting high emotion—almost a religious trance. In the songs and poems of their children they found an expression of their own inner sadness and hopes. . . . at moments like that, one was afraid to glance at the face of others, fearing that an inevitable doom of the tomorrow will look back from the eyes.[35]

It was only a small respite in a sea of terror. Yet it secretly was looked upon as an investment in the future. These children were the guarantors of the survival of the race beyond the ghettos and concentration camps. With their play, they engendered high morale, compassion, and even a faint hope for a better future. For Rudolf Vrba in Auschwitz, the scene of the newly arrived children and their play activity in the Family Camp was a source of "wonder, elation, nostalgia. . . . and somehow the sight of it was good for my morale, even though I had a nasty suspicion that those children were going to die."[36]

To many community leaders the traditional structures of social stability and order appeared to be on the brink of disintegration—and in fact they were. However, Czerniakow must have realized the sight of children at play had a calming effect upon the tense and agitated ghetto population during times of distress. The picture of smiling children at the opening of the playground on Grzybowska Street, which took place only a month before the liquidation of the Warsaw ghetto, made a more positive impact on the terrified people than scores of reassuring speeches by the chairman. Looking around, Czerniakow jotted down in his diary, "the ceremony made a great impression on those present. Balm for the wounds. The street is smiling!"

At their core, playgrounds stood as evidence of an active and conscious attempt to influence the social-psychological dimensions of a tormented community. Both Czerniakow from Warsaw and Jacob Gens from Vilna used playgrounds to maintain morale and contain panic. Were they good psychologists or just desperate men? One can only ponder. But Freud said that no one believes in his own death and one nurtures a hope for a reprieve even at the last second. In the final account, history must judge Czerniakow's attempts three days before the commencement of the final expulsion of over 300,000 Jews from Warsaw against the background of a very desperate time. The playgrounds became his last hope for containing the social and psychological collapse of the ghetto. "Incredible panic in the city," Czerniakow laconically wrote on July 19, 1942. "I drove through the streets of the entire Quarter. I visited 3 playgrounds. I do not know whether I managed to calm the population, but I did my best."[37]

AMONG THE MANY problems of Jewish camp administrations and ghetto councils, controlling the gangs of children who roamed the streets or camps unsupervised became one of the most urgent priorities. In Westerbork, some eyewitnesses and survivors noted, the young, cooped up with adults, simply ran amok, cursed and detested by their elders. The corrupting influences of the unbridled sexual promiscuity permeating camp life had obvious consequences on the morals of the children. However, the lack of any permanency in their lives had an even more devastating impact upon them. Bed-wetting, assorted nervous disorders, and hypertension became common symptoms for many. Schools, a nursery, and, after September 1943, a small playground with seesaws, horizontal bars, swings, and a sandpit were organized with the specific purpose of bringing a measure of control into the disheveled lives of the camp children.[38]

Throughout the occupied East, the already mentioned closing of schools had frighteningly similar impacts upon the social fabric of the children's world. The ever-increasing number of orphans—the consequence of the high mortality rate among the refugees—further aggravated this "youth problem." The clandestinely established educational systems succeeded in capturing only a small minority of the young. The overwhelming majority of children remained without moral guidance and physical sustenance. Issues of law and order arose in the face of a youth that showed a marked degree of demoralization. "Pitched battles between children's gangs" became a common occurrence in Warsaw. In Vilna forty children, ranging from five to fifteen, were caught and incarcerated in the ghetto jail for various offenses. The handling of the increasing number of orphans was particularly troublesome and a special youth group had to be organized for combating juvenile delinquency. A major impetus for playgrounds and supervised activities came from the simple proposition that play and exercise were wholesome, a deterrent to crime and diseases. The whole matter of these children obviously transcended the purely criminal domain and was handled with compassion, for the most part, on the local level by the Jewish Police. A much more serious matter was the conspicuous appearance of bands of "unproductive" children, who genuinely frightened communal authorities. Their apprehension was perhaps justified in the precarious ghetto existence because unsupervised groups of youth roaming the streets had the potential of igniting a violent German response, i.e., Kinderaktion, against all the children.

Playgrounds were inaugurated and play days organized as conscious efforts of controlling space, time, and behavior. The Bialystok Judenrat decided to create a playground in the summer of 1942 for children up to seven years old with these specific concerns in mind. This park served soup and bread to the youngsters and provided them with all-day play opportunities. However, the minutes of the Judenrat as well as its announcement made it clear that one motivation behind the establishment of the park was to eliminate "provocatively colorful baby-carriages" as well as aimless and unsupervised children from the streets. To quote Janina David's words again: "it was dangerous to be in the streets the whole day" in Warsaw not only during special Aktionen, but also at any period because raiding parties routinely combed the ghetto for children and the elderly. Caution prevailed everywhere. In Lodz, the head of the Judenrat ordered the establishment not only of nurseries for infants, but also of youth halls adjoining workshops where children from age eight and nine were forced to work.[39] In an appeal to the children of the ghetto, the department of education informed them about the opening of a playground, and also warned them explicitly:

> we also appeal to you not to loiter around the streets aimlessly—"walk in the straight and narrow." Do not walk and stop by the wire [fence]. . . . Whoever needs to pass the wire fence should hurry by and not be inquisitive as to what happens on the other side.
>
> Children! We believe you will conform to our fatherly advice and influence also your relatives to do likewise, because it is for our own benefit. We will thus avert, with God's help, a lot of misfortune.[40]

At face value, these efforts were also designed to provide badly needed child care for parents whose work kept them away from their homes for twelve to fourteen hours a day. Yet there was no escape from the contradictions of these irrational times. While the councils wanted to avoid incurring the wrath of the German authorities by letting children roam the ghetto streets in conspicuous number, the assembling of them into kindergartens and nurseries presented equally grave danger. Collection points like these would make the work of the police (the SS or the Gestapo) that much easier for carrying out a Kinderaktion. Thus many parents denied their children the little opportunity left for play. Often, the young remained alone for long hours, hidden in their apartment or with specific instructions in case of a Kinderaktion. These concerns based on the already mentioned raids of children's homes in Lodz and elsewhere, were well founded. Kindergartens and playgrounds became easily sprung traps when the time of deportations came. Precisely for that reason it was decided by the ghetto council of Siaulaui (Lithuania) not to establish kindergartens. It would be dangerous, to quote the secret proceedings of a meeting, "if children and a children's home should be found in the ghetto."[41]

In numerous instances the Nazi authorities themselves established children's homes as a lure to seduce children out from hiding and then deport them. In Plaszow, the feared camp commander Amon Goeth initiated the building of a special children's home and playground for almost three hundred children who had been smuggled into the camp by a variety of ways. Councillors and playground supervisors were selected from among the inmates, and grass and flower beds were planted around the whole complex. It was an inspiring sight, a miracle, for some of the children for whom "this was the first time in their short lives that they had ever seen a flower." It took only a few hours, several weeks later, to collect the same children and transport them for extermination. In the small Polish town of Wisnieze-Nowy, posters instructed the local Jews to put their children into a "Children's House." Parents, worried about the Germans' intentions, completely refused to send their children into this trap. Even young children were not fooled by this ruse. "I already understood," a boy of seven recalled after the liberation, "that the Germans wanted to trick the Jewish children into this 'children's house' and would shoot us all once we were there. All the children talked about this."[42]

Child-care institutions were easy and prominent targets for German raiding parties. The tale of Janusz Korczak's orphanage has often been told. As the German and Ukranian police surrounded the orphanage, two hundred children marched out, washed and in clean clothing, toward the collection point (Umschlagplatz) for deportation. They were singing. The "Old Doctor" walked at the head of the procession, hatless, his body broken and bent but his head raised. Korczak refused pleas that he remain in Warsaw and leave his children to their fate. "I will never forget that procession," wrote Nachum Remba, an eyewitness, as they were filing into the train that took them to Treblinka and their deaths. Remba could not control himself and he wept bitterly at Jewish helplessness.[43] History is not full of stories of poetic justice, and the history of the Holocaust has very few. A day before ending his tortuous life by taking poison, Czerniakow had to endure a final humiliation. As the first salvo in the extermination of the Warsaw ghetto, a terse entry in his diary testified that he was to witness the removal of children from the same playground that was his pride and joy, exactly opposite the community building.

While educators in orphanages and nurseries sang and played with their little wards, "taking them to a land of fairy-tales," they were haunted by soul-searching questions and burdened by the weight of their responsibility. "Only in the evening . . . we would sit and discuss this possibility [of

8. "The Liquidation of Dr. Korczak's Orphanage." Pencil drawing by Halina Olomucka, 1942–43. Courtesy of the Musée des Deux Guerres Mondiales (Paris) —BDIC (Universités de Paris).

Kinderaktion]. Surrounded by toys and paintings of the children, we asked the same question with trembling voices again and again: what will happen if they come to take them? . . . what would we say to the mothers?" When asked for a religious opinion in this case, even the rabbis found it difficult to formulate guidelines for the conscience-stricken teachers or to offer words of comfort. The parents, submerged in their own desperation, were not in a position to give relief to the educators either. They had countless other burdens to carry. A mother, working in a labor-commando, whose task was to evacuate belongings of deported families, remembered how "little dolls, toy horses, kittens and dogs stared at me. . . . On several occasions we burst into hysterical weeping at the sight of the children's toys. Our hands and legs refused to do our bidding, we could not work."[44]

PLAY ITSELF RAISED a moral dilemma that sharply divided the Jewish communities. It was hard to resolve the issue of whether play, games (even sports competitions), and occasional merriment should coexist with destruction, death, and suffering. On the one hand, there were conscious efforts made by ghettos and camps to introduce play activities into the lives of the young for reasons already elaborated. On the other hand, large segments of the population disapproved of ostentatious mirth with the rationale that "a graveyard is no place for entertainment." In light of the suffering, grief, and constant terror, their reticence is understandable. Its source was a religious and moral resistance to every form of celebration and its manifestation was a reaction against the building of playgrounds, their festive openings, and organized play days. In a fiery confrontation, the Commission of Religious Affairs in Warsaw presented Czerniakow with a petition for banning "parties or musical and singing performances" during the traditional weeks of mourning. "I said to Eckerman, who was supporting this position," Czerniakow wrote in his characteristically terse style in July 1942, "what I often repeat, that 'one cannot wind one's watch with tears' (Dickens). To which he replied that it is precisely with tears that a Jewish watch can be wound."[45] A follow-up entry a few days later revealed that Czerniakow remained undeterred by religious opposition and went ahead with a festive program for 600 children.

As significant as the religious argument may have been against merriment, the moral view as to the appropriateness of play in times of communal and individual disaster was equally weighty and divisive. To find the source of this resistance on part of both religious and secular circles, we should mention that partly in spite of and partly because of the murky future and depressing hopelessness a distinctly "hedonistic" strain emerged within adult society in many ghettos and camps. Even the severe moralist Kaplan had to admit: "There is a lot of frivolity in the ghetto, in order to somewhat lessen its sorrow." It fomented both soul-searching and strife within ghetto societies. Pain forced itself upon every aspect of life. Mechanicus from the Westerbork camp noticed, for example, that

> Many German and Dutch Jews refuse to go to the revue, the former because they find there is a painful contrast between the "fun" and the tragedy of the transports, the latter because they cannot enjoy themselves while their relatives, their wives, their husbands or their children, are suffering an unknown fate, joyless, dreary, deprived of everything.

Mechanicus found similar sentiments toward all forms of merriment, whether for adults or the young. "Families play party games, monopoly and so on," he wrote in 1943, "but in a minor key. There is always sorrow in the background—they speak again and again about members of their families who have been deported to Poland."[46]

Like every facet of life in the enclosed society of a ghetto or camp, children's play was not exempt from scrutiny. Dutch Jews, who were deported from Westerbork to Bergen Belsen, celebrated their queen's birthday by organizing festivities for the children in 1944. In all likelihood, it was a desperate attempt on the part of the adults to bring back a cherished past and provide the young with rare moments of joy. It was, also, a form of defiance in face of oppression and possibly succeeded in raising the morale of both adults and children. But we also must remember the grim statistics at the same time: this was Bergen Belsen where thousands died each day from malnutrition, exhaustion, and typhus. Hanna Levy-Haas, an inmate from Yugoslavia, and an intellectual who was intimately involved in youth welfare, could not hide her disbelief or distress. "However could they think of such a thing at a time like this? . . . I could not believe my eyes," she exclaimed in her diary.[47]

The extent of the tragedy forced other educators and civic leaders to grapple with the same issue all through Nazi-held Europe. In Vilna, where the population was sharply divided on the question of entertainment, the ghetto leadership itself banned games and sports for a whole day. For the first anniversary of the Vilna ghetto, a day of mourning was declared—both in protest and in grief. Zelig Kalmanowitch's diary recounted that "playing and singing are forbidden. Even on the field there are no games." The Jewish community of Vilna was dealt with especially harshly by the Nazi extermination squads. Over half the population was executed outright in the early stages of the occupation and Aktionen were frequent thereafter. Anything resembling joy and merriment, including children's play, was hard to justify under these circumstances. Although he did not condemn them, Kalmanowitch was at a loss to explain rationally how games could take place on the athletic field amidst the slaughter: "The games are cheered loudly—as we were free. A road to man. My pious friend laments: 'So many mourn, so many died, and here merriment and celebrations!' " The only way these two ideas could be reconciled in the mind of a Jew as pious as Kalmanowitch was through religion: "Such is life. But we must live as long as God gives life." His views reflected, as touched upon earlier, a strong undercurrent in Jewish theology and thought of the times, to respond to the Nazi plans of extermination by the sanctification of life. Though not purely instinctual, the reaction of the Jewish masses, especially in Eastern Europe, "was fundamentally what might be called 'Tzu iberleybn,' the sanctification of life, the overwhelming impulse to preserve life in the midst of death. . . ."[48]

At least Kalmanowitch could fall back on his religion. For others there was neither an easy answer nor an escape to be found; one could at best only accept one's fate with dignity. As a central player of the drama unfolding in the Warsaw ghetto, the often-maligned Adam Czerniakow understood this perhaps the best. He may have actually known, although his diary gives no clues to that effect, that his efforts to create playgrounds as a counterbalance to reality were ultimately futile. But the events of his last days show that he no longer trusted in the chances of survival:

> Many people hold a grudge against me for organizing play activity for the children, for arranging festive openings of playgrounds, for the music, etc. I am reminded of a film: a ship is sinking and the captain, to raise the spirits of the passengers, orders the orchestra to play a jazz piece. I had made up my mind to emulate the captain.[49]

If one believes contemporary descriptions, Czerniakow was not a religious man and could find neither solace nor answers in the Scriptures. Harboring no qualms or illusions about the final outcome of his labors and the inevitability of doom, he made all attempts to ameliorate the lot of children. His actions were guided, prominently, by a universal humanism and a motto borrowed from Dickens used repeatedly in his diary: "One cannot wind one's watch with tears."

4
Play and the Children

"Somewhere, far away out there,
childhood sweetly sleeps . . ."

IN A TOUCHING entry in *The Diary of a Young Girl,* Anne Frank cried out while she was standing in front of a concealed window in their hideout: "a good laugh would help more than ten Valerian pills. . . . cycling, dancing, whistling, looking out into the world, feeling young, to know that I'm free—that's what I long for." She was not asking why her existence had become one of privation and loneliness. Her comment was spontaneous—it was the outburst of an adolescent who had been denied vital elements of life, simple experiences like walking in the park, breathing the fresh air, holding hands with a friend, and just being a child.

She was not alone in her despair. Millions of children longed for a better life and hoped for a better future. Their voices echo similar sentiments through the faded pages of extant diaries and in the memories of those who survived the inferno. The descriptive power of a child's words is so vivid, so penetrating that we can almost feel, smell, and touch their palpable anguish and fear. Although muffled by a veil of pain and suffering, the words leave no doubt, either, about their writer's perceptions regarding the world, existence, and the longing for life's little pleasures. Forces beyond the children, and even beyond their elders, thrust these youngsters into an alien and perplexing universe of ghettos, camps, and hideouts, all of which made indelible marks on their minds and psyches. Although their voices are haunting, it is important to listen to the children of the Holocaust, for they saw everything that grown-ups saw. With the premonition of the condemned they told in their poems and diaries and painted in their drawings their fears.

They were honest, measuring their world in terms of immediate needs. There was a certain finality, a starkness, in their perception of this world tottering on the brink of complete moral and rational collapse.

The first and initial period, with its restricting legislation and consequent ghettoization, was perhaps the most trying for the young inhabitants of the Holocaust world. Like a tornado, the winds of war destroyed their familiar surroundings, robbed them of a world of beauty, and removed the warm and protective aura of the family. They were shoved into camps, enclosed in ghettos, and sent into hiding, sometimes with their parents and sometimes in the care of gentile protectors. All these changes presented a nightmarish world, and all had their crippling effects. As the first stage of descent into the abyss, the security and warmth of a familiar surrounding, a home, evaporated quickly into the haphazard and shiftless existence of the ghettos and camps. An unknown child in Theresienstadt wrote in his poem "Homesick":

> I've lived in the ghetto here more than a year,
> In Terezin, in the black town now,
> And when I remember my old home so dear,
> I can love it more that I did, somehow.
>
> Ah, home, home,
> Why did they tear me away?
> Here the weak die easy as a feather
> And when they die, they die forever.
>
> . . . .
>
> Yet we all hope the time will come
> When we'll go home again.
> Now I know how dear it is
> And often I remember it.[1]

In the children's exile in a strange and wretched world—ghettos, camps, and hideouts—a fundamental, extreme transformation in the quality, nature, and meaning of life took place so quickly that it shook the foundation of their emotional and intellectual universe. With the loss of their homes, the children lost the familiar little playthings, the warm blankets, and life's little amenities like a warm roll, a cup of milk, and a piece of candy. Hazy afternoons filled with the laughter and excitement of an excursion to a park, riverbank, forest, or playground became distant and tearful memories. The playing throngs of the tenement houses, congregating on the street corners, also, disappeared suddenly and irretrievably. The green meadows, the majestic crowns of green trees, and the smell of freshly cut grass—all symbolizing a rebirth and perhaps a better future—were nowhere to be found.

For the ghetto dwellers, the parks themselves presented a sight unlike that of prewar days. They were pitiful economical replicas—desert outposts with bombed-out buildings as backdrops, bare patches of greenery. Moishele, a ghetto child from Vilna, exemplified the yearnings and despair of all his contemporaries:

> There is a flower blooming outside the ghetto
> Between the fences it speaks to me:
> "Moishele, why are you still there?
> Come to me, come."[2]

Under normal circumstances it is doubtful that we even notice a handful of leaves, a few sprigs of flowers, or a tiny sparrow—they are taken for granted. However, in the ghettos and camps, where suffering and deprivation magnified everything, they came to symbolize life and their disappearance was morally debilitating. What the adults surely noticed and grieved for on an aesthetic level, the children genuinely missed, acutely feeling the void. A little girl who hid with her family in the sewers and was supplied with food by gentile sewer workers, begged them only "to bring some wild flowers." She was craving the sight of a dog or cat; her younger brother "longed for birds." These needs were instinctual and fundamental. The testimony of Genia Silkes, a former teacher in the Warsaw ghetto, also reflects the yearning of the youth of the ghetto for even the semblance of some green.

> But there was no green. One little girl, she was dying, told her sister she would like to see a leaf, to hold something green. Her sister went out, under the wall. The children would pick away bricks and go under the wall. If there was a kind Jewish policeman, they would bring in food. This little girl went to the Aryan side, to a park, and picked a little leaf. That was all. She came back through the hole and put it in a glass by her sister's bed. The other little girl lay there, sucking her thumb, smiling. And then she died."[3]

THE CHILDREN'S PERCEPTION of the significance of their environment and the opportunities it provided for play and games knew neither national boundaries nor distinction of class or age. It became almost inevitable that the adults sensed and appreciated their importance and necessity. Hanna Levy-Haas in Bergen Belsen acknowledged the nightmarish surrounding, yet noted that children's yearning for play naturally burst forth even amidst the horror. She saw it as an instinctual, an almost atavistic impulse embedded in the human consciousness: "I feel it is an urge that springs from the soul of the children themselves," she wrote in 1944, "for they follow my

9. A group of children engrossed in a game in the Lodz ghetto, 1940–42. From the Archives of the Simon Wiesenthal Center, Los Angeles, Calif.

lead in their excitement, they show their desire to live, to play, a desire stronger than they are themselves."[4]

Children formulated their views with less eloquence. Indeed, for many the measurement and understanding of the world must have been based on intuitive and cognitive processes that enabled them to place their needs of existence in order of priorities. Where play and games precisely ranked in this hierarchical order in the children's value system can only be surmised. Still, it seems valid to say that they occupied a prominent place among the psychological needs of a child. Anne Frank touchingly exemplifies the longing of many children "to have lots of fun . . . for once, and to laugh until my tummy ache[s]." The same message filters through the many pages and memories: the play activities made life's continuation possible for a little while longer by making the camps, ghettos, and the cramped hideouts somewhat more bearable.

These subconscious needs for ludic experience, not always amenable to adult logic and rationalization, manifested themselves on many levels and forms. One was artistic expression through paintings. Several thousand drawings and paintings survived Theresienstadt, and in them we see the preoccupation of their creators with the rare moments of joy in the world of play. Eli Bachner, who was deported to Theresienstadt at the age of ten, was not as eloquent as Anne Frank, yet his words convey to us, on a different level, feelings toward play similar to hers. His fondest recollections always centered on sports and games, which were organized by adults for the children: "For me the most pleasant memories are attached to the soccer games. . . . every game has turned into a conversation piece in our class for a whole week." Later, when he was thirteen, he was sent to Birkenau as a builder's apprentice. He admitted then that games and sport continued to serve as center of the children's world. Another youngster's rationale for playing soccer in the presence of the SS in Theresienstadt is almost apologetic in comparison: "we were young, and we enjoyed the Sunday afternoon games. . . ."[5]

Because it was enigmatic and contradictory, the situation at Theresienstadt is difficult to ignore. It was the only camp where the care, love, and shelter of children, as temporary as their influences on the final outcome may have been, made any dent in the psychological and physical destruction. Adults were the initiators of organized play and games, and the children recognized and appreciated these efforts. Undoubtedly, in their view these games possessed a special importance in the monotony of the camp. A young boy's admission testifies to his feeling that "the most beautiful day was for me the moment, when, as a passionate soccer player, I could don for the first time the uniform of the G.W. and fight for its honor."

Theresienstadt, with all its evil, misery, and convoluted reality, was still less forbidding than Buchenwald, Bergen Belsen, or Auschwitz, but children almost everywhere responded to the destruction of their familiar universe by creating a new world or reformulating the old one. It seems that in the early stages of the Holocaust, the younger generation relied to a large extent on adult initiatives to create a play world for them. Later, the forced separation of families and the loss of parents, relatives, classmates, friends, and teachers prompted many of the children to recognize the importance of self-reliance and motivation. In a Jewish paper, *Gazeta Zydowska,* issued under close German scrutiny in the Cracow ghetto, a little girl named Martha published this poem:

I must be saving these days
(I have no money to save),
I must save health and strength,
Enough to last me for a long while.
I must save my nerves,
And my thoughts, and my mind,
And the fire of my spirit;
I must be saving of the tears that flow—

I shall need them for a long, long while.
I must save endurance these stormy days.

There is so much I need in my life:
Warmth and feeling and a kind heart—
These things I lack; of these I must be saving!
All these, the gifts of God,
I wish to keep.
How sad I should be
If I lost them quickly.[6]

This philosophy of self-preservation was especially valuable in circumstances when a child was isolated from extended human contact. The most traumatic and damaging psychological experience for a child was a hermetic quarantine from sun, air, and open spaces and from the sound of laughter. In the Warsaw ghetto, boys and girls "would longingly peek through the cracks and holes in the ghetto walls to get a glimpse of the trees and flowers that grew on the 'other side.' " The sense of isolation was even more acute for those who were forced into years of hiding under the most trying circumstances. A seven-year-old girl, whose family hid in the city sewers of Lvov (Lemberg), had not seen sunshine for more than a year. Propelled by an irresistible urge, she went into a pipe to look out at the world. "I only felt a little bit of fresh air." She reminisced on that years later. "I craved so much for the sun and fresh air that I cannot describe it. I could hear cars drive past right on top of us, I heard people's voices and the gay laughter of children playing. I often thought how happy I would be if only I could play like they did."[7]

The same theme recurs in other diaries and memoirs. Although sunshine, fresh air, and unrestricted movement are a natural, taken-for-granted part of life for a free person, they become features of a land of fairy tales for children in hiding. It was simply hard for a young child to grapple with why "there was no daylight—not even a single ray of sunlight. . . . A drop of sunlight is what I missed so much."[8] Only in their imaginations could they wander freely through the landscape of flowers inhabited by friends. It was not always a sad and forlorn world, for the little prisoners could play and share their innermost thoughts with an old worn toy. Sometimes a pair of scissors with a cardboard box meant a whole world. But it was an existence void of laughter. Condensed in a young girl's words, written in hiding, one can discover a craving not only for the expanses of the outdoors but also for other children:

> Standing behind the curtained window, I watched the children playing and wished that I too could go outside. Instead I visited the children on paper: I took a walk with them on paper.

10. Crayon drawing of children in play, from an anonymous diary from Theresienstadt. Courtesy of Precious Legacy Project, Linda Altschuler, B'nai B'rith Klutznik Museum, Washington, D.C.

> Small green leaves covered the trees and sun-shine splashed the streets. Spring was greeting Lwow [Lvov], casting warm shadows on crowded P Square. Little girls' boots were replaced by shoes, scarves were discarded, jackets were opened. The children's laughter matched the weather. A balloon floated past our window and almost touched the bricks.[9]

For some like this little girl, the presence of a family member ameliorated, in some degree, their depressing experiences. It had no power to guarantee any measure of physical protection, but the close proximity and comforting presence of parents and siblings provided an emotional curtain of security. That was not the case with abandoned or hidden youngsters under the care of others. Indeed, the most psychologically vulnerable were those children who stayed in hiding with families who cared for them for monetary rewards. A little boy, who was hidden in a cupboard and under a bed for years and could not walk at the age of six, knew of the capture and execution of his father. In describing his ordeal after the liberation, he also recalled that when his "protector's" "elder daughter had gone to play outside I wanted to cry, for I envied her. It was already three to four years that I hadn't gone out of doors."[10]

These yearnings were not always wrapped in beautifully composed sentences or even in a coherent and rational cloak of logic. But then, even scholars and play theorists have found it difficult to formulate commonly accepted theories to explain this desire for play, except to guess that it stems from the subconscious domain of the human mind. Be that as it may, these spontaneous outbursts betray, on the part of the children, a recognition of the significance and role of parks, playgrounds, and play opportunities in their lives. While it all added up to a trying period for the children, we must differentiate between the initial stages of German occupation, which were sometimes relatively benign periods, and the final road to destruction which represented a swift and lethal spiral toward death. Both stages presented the children with bewildering contradictions, but in both phases children played. Also, in both stages the paradoxes of their precarious existence in ghettos, camps, and hideouts reveal the complexion and contradictions of a convoluted society.

It is worth noting that open dance halls in the Warsaw ghetto coexisted with frightful naturality with carts collecting corpses lying on the sidewalks. "In the daytime, when the sun is shining, the ghetto groans. But at night everyone is dancing even though his stomach is empty," remarked Kaplan. The contradictions did not end here. At the same time that decrees excluded Jews from city parks, German soldiers were willing to play soccer against ghetto children. With his sharp eye for the absurd in ghetto life, Kaplan recorded the ultimate paradox—a moment of truce on the playing field:

> On one of the empty lots in Gesia Street several Jewish boys organized some sort of athletic game; some German soldiers noticed it. When they passed the lot, they addressed the players courteously and asked for permission to join their game. The youths agreed. After the game was over they parted like friends and comrades. It was a miracle. And that is not all.
>
> There was a case in which some Jewish boys were seized for forced labor and transported to their place of work. But instead of work, they were invited to play soccer, and to the Aryans' distress they were beaten by the children of the "inferior race." But they were not humiliated, and for revenge they set a time for playing another game.

For the contemporaries it was hard to rationalize these occurrences and everyone considered them as true miracles. (Indeed, we are hard pressed to find an explanation for this paradox even today.) Experiences like that were so rare that Kaplan in Warsaw had to grapple for words to explain this touch of humanity. Ringelblum, who also noticed or heard rumors of a friendly game between Jews and Germans, wrote in his diary sometime later that "the Jews won 2 to 1. It's characteristic that when alone individual Germans behave humanely."[11]

It is obvious that this behavior was more of an exception (an aberration) than the rule, and it may be attributed to the fact that both the children and their executioners had not yet begun their final descent, on their different paths, toward the abyss of inhumanity. Of all the play experiences it is the concept and even the notion of children's play in the extermination camps that most tax the rationality of the human mind and imagination. The human mind is not always able to comprehend or assimilate the coexistence of atrocity and death and child's play. The first snow of the winter of 1943–44 in Birkenau, the epitome of a death camp, brought to some fortunate youngsters a rare opportunity to play. "Skating fans, old and new, had all the slippery streets to compete upon. Tougher lads recalled their childhood with snowball fights."[12] It must not have been an isolated phenomenon. Since these children were fourteen and fifteen years old and already accepted as regular slave laborers, they had some, though limited, freedom in expressing their youthful energies.

A special place must be devoted to the existence of children's play, though unwitting, during the final stages of the extermination process. Indeed, play burst forth spontaneously and uncontrollably without regard to the external situation. Children on their way to the gas chambers were not always aware what awaited them at the end of the dusty road. Yet even amidst the surrealistic landscape of death, in the extermination centers, the fluttering presence of rare moments of a child forgetting or ignoring the ever-present death is real. Among the many painful scenes, there were unique instances when the prisoners, and sometimes even their executioners, stood with tears in their eyes watching a playing child entering the gas chamber. Children spent their precious last moments in play—oblivious to the shadows of the gas chambers and the crematoriums. Disguised by an idyllic grove, the extermination facilities in Auschwitz/Birkenau were often the backdrop for a child's smile, a small hand reaching out for a flower, or a mother caringly adjusting a bow in the well-combed hair of a little girl. Many of the mothers, themselves exhausted from the ordeal of the deportation, could not conceive the inevitability of the end. One reads in Kitty Hart's book, *I Am Alive,* how she and other Auschwitz prisoners of a work unit, whose task it was to sort out the clothing of the dead, witnessed the combination of atrocity and play in almost disbelief. Yet, while all around them were screams, "death, smoking chimneys making the air black and heavy with soot and the smell of burning bodies," children succeeded in stealing

11. Hungarian children before their death playing in the birch grove surrounding the gas chamber. Courtesy of the Simon Wiesenthal Center, Los Angeles, Calif.

an instant of joy. Hart and others lived in a hut near the crematoria and witnessed the endless columns of passing women

> poor and rich, tired looking, clutching their children and babies. Sometimes a small child wheeled a doll in a little pram, or jumped over a skipping rope. A mother would change a baby while waiting or put a bonnet over a child's head lest the sun would be too hot for it. A child would pick up a flower which grew near the road. . . .[13]

It is not hard to authenticate this tragic scene. Indeed, there are numerous diaries and testimonies describing the heart-rending scenes of children who played in the "portal of death." Such an extraordinary moment became etched in the memory of Erik Kulka, an author and himself an Auschwitz survivor. In an attempt to distract and calm down her five-year-old daughter in the waiting area adjacent to the gas chambers, a mother, knowing full well their bitter fate, begged her to dance "one more little dance before we will unite with grandma." People who were waiting for their death suddenly forgot the stench of burning flesh and the tears of fellow victims as

> children and women arranged themselves around the beautifully dancing little girl in a place which can be properly termed as the "Waiting Room of Death." Even some of the SS men were taken by surprise and followed the motions of the little dancer with interest.
>
> She never finished her little routine. Kramer [the commandant] entered the room suddenly shouting: "This is no place for theatrical performances," and ordered them to enter the gas chamber.[14]

These were perplexing moments for all—even for the executioners. If one were to believe and give credence to the confessions of Rudolf Hoess, the commandant of Auschwitz, even he was not completely immune to some feelings of a vague humanity and, maybe, a semblance of compassion. As the commandant of the largest death factory, Auschwitz/Birkenau, he personally oversaw the killing of millions of children and adults. In a moment of remorse he recalled:

> Once two little children were so engrossed in their play that they did not want to be torn away at all from it by their mother. Even the Jews of the Sonderkommando did not want to take up the children. I will never forget the pleading look of the mother, begging for mercy though she certainly knew what was to happen. The people in the [gas] chamber were beginning to get restless—I had to act. Everyone looked at me—I gave the acting subordinate a nod, and he took the children, who were resisting strongly, into his arms and brought them to the gas chamber together with the mother, whose weeping would break one's heart. I wanted to disappear off the face of the earth out of compassion—but I was not allowed to show the slightest feeling.[15]

THESE CHILDREN, unaware of their impending fate, were perhaps the more fortunate ones. Others, before being caught by periodical German sweeps or perishing on the streets, had already seen and experienced the prolonged agony of ghetto and camp existence. For ghetto and camp children death assumed a natural and integral part of their living. In their case it is harder to explain the abundance of play because they were so acutely aware of the horrors that surrounded them and the imminence of death. With drastic curtailment of freedom, oppressive legislations, and steadily worsening circumstances in which children lived, their games and play underwent a dramatic and irrevocable metamorphosis. Their activities became governed, more and more, by the prevailing sociopsychological and economic factors that forced the children to alter and invent their own pursuits and pastimes. Indeed, children were intensely affected by the transition from freedom to physical and mental segregation, but they reacted and rebounded, on the whole, faster and more creatively than the adults. Be it in camps, ghettos, or hiding, the mental and physical constraints imposed upon the imprisoned population were the main determinants of the play experiences of children. They shaped and molded all areas of human endeavors, sparing neither the adults nor the children. Thus the physical surroundings, coupled with hunger, mental anguish, and incessant terror, stamped their impression upon every aspect of the young prisoners' existence. The games, plays, and pastimes came to reflect, inevitably, these altered conditions. To cope with the demands of their new environment and circumstances, both adults and children had to adjust, accommodate, improvise, innovate, and create a new world from scratch.

A journey into the play and recreational pursuits of children in the darkest corners of the Holocaust offers a fascinating array of experiences, episodes, and vignettes. It can illuminate the heroic and the timid, the innocent and the cunning. If we consider the extremes in their existence, the adaptability of the young seems remarkable. In the forced removal of families into ghettos and camps the material possessions that could be taken were severely circumscribed, and this necessarily included a limit on playthings. Toys were also lost and mislaid during successive moves, and the valuable ones were often confiscated by the Germans themselves or their native hirelings. In the early stages of the Theresienstadt camp, for example, no play implements came in with the stream of detainees. It took a long time before the toddlers got used to playing again because new toys had to be invented and new games had to be organized. These factors forced the children to create new play opportunities with scraps of rag or a bit of wood.[16]

These efforts by youth to create a "play world" was in evidence in every hideout and every ghetto or camp and was fostered also, to a large measure, by the absence of parental supervision that could establish a stable environment. A young girl who was hiding in Italy described a fantastic play world she could create with the help of a pair of scissors and a cardboard box. In moving from hideout to hideout, another youngster had to build toys out of mud: "boats, cannons, tanks and bunkers—all from my imagination. In this way it was easier for me to make time pass more quickly."[17] In the ghettos children created games collectively. In attempting to provide a balanced picture of ghetto life, Oskar Rosenfeld recorded in the official chronicle of the Lodz ghetto, under the heading "The Ghetto Children's Toys," that cigarette boxes became prized treasures for the children, the majority of whom had to work, at the time, in ghetto workshops and armament industries. "Children's eyes beg for those boxes, children's hands reach out for them," he wrote in July of 1943.

> Outside the ghetto, children receive beautiful and appropriate playthings as presents. There is a great industry for manufacturing them; artists and artisans invent new toys and build little altars for children's hearts out of wood, cardboard, metal, silk, and plaster. . . . A fantastic world emerges, and children go strolling through it. The children of the ghetto, however, are not blessed with such good fortune. They have to create their toys themselves. Still, the Jewish child is talented enough to do without the fantasies of the toy manufacturer. Our children collect empty cigarette boxes. They remove the colorful tops and stack them in a pile, until they have a whole deck of cards. Playing cards.
>
> And they play. They count the cards and deal them out. They arrange them by color and name. Green, orange, yellow, brown, even black. They play games that they invent for themselves, they devise systems, they let their imaginations take over.[18]

The inventiveness and fortitude of the ghetto children surprised and impressed adult society as other descriptions from Lodz testify. In retrospect, it is obvious that ghetto games and play activities were a natural reflection of a newly emerging ghetto culture and folklore. This culture amalgamated old values and traditions with the altered social and psychological conditions, creating very distinct forms of humor, songs, and poems. Children's toys, games, and play also went through a drastic transformation that could not escape the attention of contemporaries who thought these changes important enough to include them in the official ghetto chronicle. In the summer of 1943 an interesting fad captured the fancy of the same children whose musical instruments had been previously confiscated by the Gestapo. Oskar Rosenfeld, the same sharp-eyed observer of the ghetto folklore, jotted down that

> For several days now, the streets and courtyards of the ghetto have been filled with a noise like the clatter of wooden shoes.
>
> The noise is disturbing at first, but one gradually gets used to it and says to oneself: this is as much a part of the ghetto as are cesspools. The observer soon discovers that this "clattering" is produced by boys who have invented a pastime, an entertainment. More precisely, the children of the ghetto have invented a new toy.
>
> All the various amusing toys and noisemakers—harmonicas, hobby horses, rattles, building blocks, decalls, etc.—are things our youngsters must, of course, do without. In other ways as well, as ghetto dwellers, they are excluded from all the enchantments of the

12. In the ghetto children invented their own games and toys. Lodz ghetto, 1942. Courtesy of the Ghetto Fighters' Museum, Israel.

child's world. And so, on their own, they invent toys to replace all the things that delight children everywhere and are unavailable here.

The ghetto toy in the summer of 1943: Two small slabs of wood —hardwood if possible! One slab is held between the forefinger and the middle finger, the other between the middle finger and the ring finger. . . . The resulting noise resembles . . . to use musical terms, the clicking of castanets. The harder the wood, the more piercing and precise the clicking, the more successful the toy, and the greater the enjoyment. Naturally, the artistic talent of the toy carver and performer can be refined to a very high level. . . .

The streets of the Litzmanstadt ghetto [Lodz] are filled with clicking, drumming, banging. . . . Barefoot boys scurry past you, performing their music right under your nose, with great earnestness, as though their lives depended on it. . . .

A conversation with a virtuoso: "We get the wood from the Wood Works Department, but only the hardest wood is good enough."—"What is the toy called?"—"It's called a castanet. . . . I do not know why. Never heard the name before. We paint the toy to make it look nicer. That guy over there," he pointed to a barefoot boy who was sitting in the street dust, ragged and dirty, "doesn't know how to do it. You have to swing your whole hand if you want to get a good tune out. Hard wood and a hefty swing—those are the main things." A few boys gathered, clicked their castanets, and all hell let loose. It was the first castanet concert I had ever attended.

The chronicler assumes that the clicker music will vanish "after it's run its course" and be replaced by some other sort of music. But he may be wrong.[19]

ALTHOUGH GHETTOS WERE places of untold human misery, they still provided framework for human interaction with at least minimal emotional and physical support. When there was no material support, friends could create an environment for play. A five-year-old child from Kielce, Shamus, who was forced to move with his mother several times, had "no toys . . . and made do with the remnant of a broom in their crowded room or played 'going to work' with the other children of the courtyard." It will be shown later that this was one of the major differentiating elements between adult and child play. For the moment it seems reasonable to say that adult play is a well-planned and well-executed activity—it has a special and well-defined purpose and rationale. Trapped in a chronic powerlessness, adult play represented an important escape and coping mechanism both in the emotional and mental realms. Children, on the other hand, are rarely, if at all, concerned with intellectualization of their actions, especially play. Ludic experience is an innate part of their behavior. A young girl, who was asked how could she play in Auschwitz, looked at her interviewer, "her face lit up with amazement, and exclaimed: 'But I played! I played there with nothing! With the snow! With the balls of snow!' "[20]

Other youngsters, isolated from human contact, were able to devise new games and toys. A child's imagination possesses amazing powers for creating or reshaping new worlds. A three-year-old girl's recollection about hiding in a hole underground, covered with planks, reveals the predicament of children left without the amenities of life, like friends and toys. "We slept on wooden planks covered with straw. I would amuse myself by chasing the rats and mice, or by rolling stones across the floor." Gabriele Silten, a young German girl who went through both Westerbork and Theresienstadt, describes similar experiences with the greater eloquence of a ten-year-old:

> In the spaces between these beams [in the attics] lived rats with their families. We would walk on the beams to get to the spaces where the rat-families lived (or sometimes just to walk on the beams) and then

poke at them with a stick and watch them jump. Surprisingly, they never harmed us or attacked us at all."[21]

It is not difficult to detect in many of these games the element of imagination which played a striking role in their psychic world. Gabriele Silten also remembered how she and her younger friend Hans used to stand in the open arches of these attics "and pretend that we could fly. . . . The flying fantasy was lovely, though, because if we could fly, then we could fly away." Others invented imaginary friends—for example Anne Frank's "Kitty"—with whom they could share their experiences. It was natural that a child wished to be surrounded by a magic circle, a circle of friends, in which one could live another life, a life somewhat unconnected with the misery of the ghetto. These imagined friendships were not to facilitate an escape from reality, but to help to adjust to, or assist in rationalizing, a completely irrational universe. In some measure, the ghetto playgrounds, schools, and clubs served this rationalizing purpose for the ghetto youths. But children in hiding, with minimal human contact, had to invent imaginary worlds for themselves. With the aid of make-believe one could symbolically demolish the physical confines of a little room or bunker. A survivor recalled that during the first stage of their hiding her father spent long hours in their shelter telling wonderful stories. "His story telling was a life-saving, because it gave me an incredible gift." Later, when they became separated, the five-year-old relived these stories "with castles, princes and princesses. . . . I found myself living in those fantasies that my father told me. I found myself sort of losing myself in pretending to be there. And that was very useful."[22]

While play activities alternately magnified and brought into focus the reality of the situation, play and recreational pursuits could also assume a larger than normal role in a child's emotional universe. Mechanicus recorded that in the balmy September weather of Westerbork "young people are going up and down on the seesaws and swings till late in the evening. Some children were still playing there at half past nine tonight, in the bright moonlight." Thousands of miles away, in Theresienstadt, other little prisoners played with the same intensity: "anyone who witnessed those days of horror and despair will understand that the small pleasures of life were essential to counterbalance this misery." The rare moments of joy were savored, cherished, and greeted with exhilaration by the children as if they were precious presents that would not last. In an existence of perpetual flux and dangers, extremes came to be expected. For a young girl a promise of a rare theatrical performance meant a whole world: "I thought at first that the excess of happiness would make me explode like an over-filled balloon. I could not contain it. I jumped, threw myself on the beds, kicked my legs in the air and laughed aloud, and still the unbearable joy mounted inside. . . . It was indescribable. One could only shout and dance about it."[23]

Children exhibited the same intensely fiery relationship toward their toys. Toys were few and precious, so their owners became protective, possessive, and careful of them. A parent whose apartment was repeatedly ransacked and looted by Germans on the prowl for Jewish valuables remembered with genuine amazement that at one time his three-year-old son responded to the demands of the intruders "clutching his hobbyhorse by the neck, fear in his eyes . . . , 'This is my horse and you can't have him.' " In times of uncertainty and danger children instinctively drew closer to a favored toy, doll, or teddy bear. It quickly became a part of their immediate family and had to be preserved and sheltered. Before her deportation to Westerbork, Gabriele Silten entrusted her most favored bear to her gentile friend who was to return it after the war. Her two grandparents had already commited suicide back in Germany and she did not want to endanger Brunette, the bear, by taking it into the unknown. "I think the idea behind this," she recalled, "was that I did not want anything to happen to Brunette; she was too precious. Therefore I would not take her because, although we did not know where we were going, it could only be a bad place."[24]

Because only a scant number of toys filtered into ghettos and camps with the children, a hobbyhorse or a favored doll inevitably became the center of a child's universe. The toy offered not only a source of entertainment but also sorely needed emotional security. With the dwindling opportunities for play and new toys, an emotional attachment between children and their toys evolved with an intensity that surprised even the parents. The tense moments in the ghettos, camps, and hiding were the true test of how much the uprooted children needed their toys for emotional security. As a direct result of the painful loss of family members and friends, human beings who were disappearing rapidly from their lives, children's psychic lives turned more inward or toward their favored toys. A psychological transference process took place when the children could provide and perceive they were receiving love from an inanimate object instead of a loved one. They could share their fear, sorrow, anguish, love—a whole range of human emotions—for the worn-out dolls and broken toys were good listeners. The little owners could confide in them their secrets, as the plaint of an anonymous little girl expressed in a brief poem, "I Sit With My Doll":

> I sit with my dolls by the stove and dream.
> I dream that my father came back,
> I dream that my father is still alive.

13. Children with their toys lining up for deportation in a transit center in Amsterdam, 1942–43. Courtesy of Rijksinstituut voor Oorlogsdocumentatie.

> How good it is to have a father.
> I do not know where my father is.[25]

Although the ghetto had the power to incarcerate the body, it could not clip the wings of imagination. Of course, a child's imagination was limited because it could reformulate only those concepts that were known previously. Rachel Auerbach recorded in her diary of the Warsaw ghetto the futility of a conversation between two girls of eleven and five. It broke down because the younger child could not visualize a picture of swans on a beautiful lake. This went beyond fairy tales for the younger girl who had never seen in her short life either graceful swans or a crystal-blue lake. Also, an inevitable repression of previous experiences might influence fundamentally a child's power of recollection. When his mother asked David Wolf in their hiding place to make a picture of their former house, garden, the sky, and the sun the seven-year-old countered that he "had forgotten what the sky and the sun looked like."[26]

Not all were affected as drastically by their environment. A child's mind had a formidable ability to lift him or her above the ruined houses, the dirty crooked streets, the rats, the corpses, and the ever-present hunger. Together with their little inanimate friends, they could cry, grieve, and long for the departed; thus an emotional bond was created between child and toy. Ettie, a five-year-old from the ghetto of Lodz, was remembered by her nurse as a sweet girl who lost all her family. The whole tragedy of the Holocaust is condensed in her few words as "she hugged her rag doll still closer to her heart and spoke to it in a serious voice:"

> "Don't cry, my little doll. When the Germans come to grab you, I won't leave you. I'll go with you, like Rosie's mother. . . ."
>
> Having said these words she stood up and wiped away her own tears with the hem of her apron, as well as the "tears" of her doll-child, and spoke to it again in the same sad voice.
>
> "Come, I'll put you to bed. I haven't any more bread for you. You've eaten today's ration, finished, I must leave the rest for tomorrow."[27]

NOT ONLY WERE new games invented; traditional ones assumed new meaning in the lives of the young, and some of the changes point to the detrimental role of a drastically altered environment. Although we will elaborate on this theme later, it is enough to note here that these activities and their content, purpose, and rationale took on dimensions not normally associated with the conventional interpretation of play. Everything was etched in the immediate cultural and social conditions prevailing in the Holocaust.

> The realities of Ghetto life became the normal existence for children who did not know any other way of living; and so they made up songs and games where action, blockade, sorrow, tears, and hunger became ordinary vocabulary of their make believe. . . .

The children's play experiences varied predictably from place to place and time to time, since all life occurrences in the Holocaust were functionally dependent on place, time, and the socioeconomic status of the participants. Yet these variations were more of degree than substance. Basically, a frightful uniformity reigned in the depiction of Holocaust life. Nothing could escape the inquisitive eyes of children, and their minds recorded and interpreted everything in their environment. We cannot provide a more succinct description of the children's games than that of Mark Dworzecki, a Holocaust survivor and historian from Vilna: "Children in the ghetto knew what a ghetto was, and even knew the meaning of the words 'action,' 'death transport,' 'Nazi,' 'SS-man,' 'bunker' and 'partisan.' They would play at 'actions,' 'blowing up bunkers,' 'slaughtering,' and 'seizing the clothes of the dead.' "[28]

Play activities thus came to provide everywhere a naturally reflective mirror of all the sorrows, dramas, and absurdities of the children's brief existence. Indeed, the dark shadows of reality inhabited even the magic world of make-believe. A participant in these games, Tzvia Kuretzka, matter-of-factly recorded that almost all the games reflected life in the ghetto. Among the most popular ones in Vilna was "Going Through the Gate," a game that enacted the experience of thousands of Jewish laborers who, returning from forced labor, were searched by the Jewish and German police, an experience similar to running the gauntlet. The game was eerily accurate as the few Vilna survivors might recall. Two main characters were selected; Levas, the hated head of the Jewish gate guards, and Franz Murer, one of the most murderous Gestapo men. The rest of the children played the Jewish workers who tried to smuggle some food into the starving ghetto and the guards who attempted to find the contraband. While the Jewish gate guards search everyone "Murer" comes, which propels the Jewish police to intensify its brutality and, at the same time, precipitates a tumult and panic among the "workers." They try desperately to toss away the small food packages, but "Murer" finds some with the incriminating evidence and the "workers" are put aside and later are whipped by the police.[29]

Games closely resembling this scene, and involving mostly boys, were enacted in almost every ghetto. Little girls' play differed in that it enacted the female realm of ghetto life. Girls in the Lodz ghetto imitated their mothers by pretending to stand in line, clutching in their hands "Ghetto-Rumkis" (ghetto currency or coupons issued by Chaim Rumkowski, head of the Lodz Judenrat) for rations of vegetables. They replayed the scene with faithful realism. They quarreled in the queue, pushed with their elbows, and fought while pressing forward to the make-believe window. Their teacher, watching their play unobtrusively, remembered that a "blonde girl with short stiff plaits and a long, skinny face screamed: 'What a disaster! What a calamity! They swindled me, those robbers! They gave me rotten potatoes, the whole lot. What will I feed my children' "[30]

Boys' activities concentrated more on war games, as in the description from Lodz: "The 'Russians' looked aggressive, with their 'rifles' aimed, ready to start a 'battle' with the 'Germans.' . . . a handsome young boy aged not more than eight commanded 'Achtung! Left, right, left, right. . . .' " But their games were not void of ghetto influences either; exactly the opposite was true. On several occasions, the children refused to portray the hated German soldiers. The power structure of the ghetto provided them perhaps more creative intricacies for their play. An example was the game of "Eldest of the Jews," an obvious reference to Rumkowski. The child who played the title role exhibited all the negative mannerisms and duplicity of his model. He made speeches, distributed favors to those loyal to him, and punished his opponents.

> The boys applauded and laughed loudly. Soon the young "Rumkowski" began dictating to everyone.
>
> His "subjects," however, were not happy with him. They did not want to obey. Everyone demanded something "urgent" of the "Eldest." One screamed that he was sick and needed medicines, another begged not to be "deported" while a third tugged at his coat and asked for additional "privileges."
>
> The young ruler was surrounded by noises and screams. Everyone pushed forward, each child tried to be nearer the "Eldest," but he started hitting out with one of his sticks, left and right.[31]

Most of the recreational pursuits involved, naturally, a representative cross section of the children's society in the ghettos or camps. For example, hide-and-seek was suitable for every age and gender, and the "small, dirty, and foul-smelling courtyards," as a Vilna youngster termed them, were ideal places to play that game. The many little nooks and crannies of the rundown yards provided a child with ample places to hide. However, the ghetto changed both the name and nature of this innocent pastime of happier memories. It came to be known as "blockade," mimicking the roundup of Jewish children in which whole blocks were hermetically sealed off by German forces with their Jewish and native helpers. The game started off with the closing of all doors and exits. Then, according to the authentic description of an eight-year-old participant,

> Part of the children became "policemen" and part "German." The third group was comprised of "Jews" who were to hide in make-believe bunkers; that is under chairs, tables, in barrels and garbage cans. The highest distinction went to the child who played Kommandant Kitel, the Head of the Gestapo. He was always the strongest boy or girl. If a dressed-up "policeman" happened to find "Jewish" children, he handed them over to the "Germans."[32]

GHETTO AND CAMP existence also provided the children with powerful stimuli for "unconventional" social behavior. This suggests that in the ecological setting created by the Holocaust, external forces overshadowed any internally motivated influences of moderation. The brutal intrusion of the Holocaust into the lives of the adults shattered, in turn, the serenity of children's world. It was swift and deadly, destroying the natural cycle, rhythm, and moral fabric of life. Boys in the ghettos gathered into street gangs which, to quote a young girl from Warsaw, "fought ferocious battles on the stairs and I was only too glad to keep away from them." Emmanuel Ringelblum, the often-quoted social historian of the same city, addressed the problem from an adult's point of view: "The children are speedily becoming demoralized," he wrote in August 1941. "Illustrative of this tendency are the pitched battles between children's gangs, in which prisoners are taken."[33]

Although watching this behavior was a bewildering experience for a humanist like Ringelblum and might be just as puzzling to many of us today, the children's gangs and their behavior are unexpected only in a conventional hierarchy of human values. The Holocaust, however, exemplified the banality of the unconventional and irrational. What the children did was not divorced from reality. In fact, play was, as was intimated in somewhat more nebulous terms earlier, an intricate part of reality—a reflective mirror that often returned a picture in a distorted form. Play provided the children with "a buffered learning," an activity frame in which one could learn to be safe in an abnormal situation, without worrying about being out of control. Thus children took into their lives naturally even the death that surrounded them. In spite of their elders' desperate efforts to shelter them from the atrocities, their games in the ghettos and camps reflected, inevitably, the surrounding horror. Death became a central theme in their precarious and short lives for it enveloped them on every side. Again, Ringelblum's description of the Warsaw ghetto, which with all its horrors was less forbidding than a death camp, shed piercing light on the situation of the ghetto child. "The children are no longer afraid of death. In one courtyard, the children played a game tickling a corpse."[34]

The games of children prisoners in concentration camps were even more symptomatic of this moral deterioration when all the tragedy of the younger generation was enacted in play. Although human logic cannot easily assimilate this fact, the Holocaust supplies us with ample documentation that play can take place at any time and any place. The children in the Ravensbrueck concentration camp for women differed little from other terrorized and traumatized ones. Because the camp was set up exclusively for women, a few mothers succeeded in bringing children with them—especially after 1944 when the rigid rules against unproductive elements (i.e., children) became somewhat more lax. One of the eminent prisoners of the camp was Emma Gluck–La Guardia, the sister of the staunchly anti-Nazi mayor of New York—a fact that perhaps saved her life. She and her daughter and grandson were deported to this notorious camp. In her memoirs she estimated that there were pehaps 500 little children living at the camp in 1944. "They looked like skeletons wearing rugs. Some had no hair on their heads. Nevertheless, they behaved like children, running around and begging things from their elders. They even played games. A popular one was Appel, modeled on the camp's daily roll calls."[35]

Play was an integral part of life, even in the most inhumane extermination centers such as Auschwitz/Birkenau. For example, hitting each other became play for the Greek boys in Birkenau.

> They called it "Klepsi Klepsi"—a nickname to stealing. The harder you slapped your blindfolded playmate's face the more fun there would be in watching him try to recognize you from among the crowd of grinning bystanders, all doing their best to look guilty, and if he did, it was your turn to cover up your eyes and guess who was hitting you.

The game itself, if we try to understand its meaning, is an interesting summation of camp life with its unique values and code of ethics. Both the stealing and the beating was rooted in the present reality. One of the most important aspects of survival in any camp was an inmate's ability illegally to procure more food than the meager ration that, by itself, meant a sentence of slow death by starvation. The procurement of food was veiled in euphemistic terms, such as "organizing," "borrowing," and "pinching." While in today's norms and under today's circumstances these acts might be considered immoral, they made it possible to live. Thus many in the camp would not condemn stealing, even though a stolen portion meant less food for somebody else. It was only the answer to want and privation, but if one was caught the punishment almost always carried savage beatings.[36]

The suffocating and frightening surrealistic landscape of death, we must emphasize again and again, was nowhere more evident than in Auschwitz. It stamped its ghoulish presence not only upon the children's psyche, but on every human endeavor as well. Death took place everywhere; it appeared in every shape. A nurse in one of the children's blocks of Auschwitz/Birkenau reported that some of the bigger boys played games of daring. They approached the electric fence, some even quickly touching it with the tips of their fingers. They generally were lucky because the current was shut off during the day. The children were especially aware of the presence of death when they saw pillars of fire rising up daily from the chimneys of the crematoria and they used these symbols of death in their games.

> They played "Lageraeltester" and "Blockaeltester," "Roll Call," shouting "Caps off!" They took on the roles of the sick who fainted during roll call and were beaten for it, or they played "Doctor"—a doctor who would take away food rations from the sick and refuse them all help if they had nothing to bribe him with. . . . Once they even played "Gas Chamber." They made a hole in the ground and

threw in stones one after the other. Those were supposed to be people put in the crematoria, and they imitated their screams. They wanted me to show them how to set up the chimney.[37]

This picture, as striking a point as it might seem to make about the "moral deterioration" of the youth, only represents the larger society revolving around it. One is almost reluctant to use the pejorative term *moral deterioration* to characterize the behavior of the children who were so obviously victims. Their actions represent a fraying of the moral fiber of society only by pre- and post-Holocaust values and norms. At the time, the children's behavior was as normal as the governing environment decreed it to be. It was a reflection of a camp culture that, just like the ghettos, possessed a very distinct and unique set of rules, and those rules were not governed by the ordinary values, norms, or codes of conduct of a normal civilization. It was a part of a painful "cultural" clash that took place between whatever vague parental influence remained from a faded and almost mythical past, an influence that attempted to shelter and protect the children, and the immediate reality.

The contradictions were enormous. The medium that could create a vague and tenuous bridge over the abyss between a hazy past and a stark presence was the games and play activities springing up spontaneously even in the middle of Auschwitz. They helped the children assimilate the horrors on their own terms and accommodate their psychic universe to the environment. It was perhaps not a coincidence that almost no suicide was recorded among children or teenagers, in contrast to that of the adult population. One of the likely reasons for this anomaly was that these children possessed an ability and imagination, which were rarely found among adults, to enact atrocity through play. A certain quality of accommodation, without compromising integrity, was the main spring of this tendency to "play out reality." These activities became an important means for the children to make sense of a world that, although it contradicted the values of their parents, was frightfully familiar and immediate to them. Their elders were not as pliant. They could not shape their new world by the sheer power of imagination. They had either to devise an "escape mechanism" or to break both physically and mentally. One of the most lucid and tragic summations of the moral agony and powerlessness of the adults in the face of reality was made by a mother at the end of her emotional tether: "This is no life; it's a chess game, in which you play the white pieces and the black pieces at the same time."[38]

5
Play and the Human Spirit

"Every dance is a protest against our oppressors"

FRIEDRICH SCHILLER'S WORDS of two hundred years ago sound commandingly pertinent to children's play in the Holocaust: "A man only plays when he is human in the fullest sense of the word and he is only human in the fullest sense of the word when he plays." With this remark the incomparable German poet succeeded in capturing the essence of play, seeing it as more than the incidental or insignificant occurrence and frivolous activity in human development that it has been construed and pictured as being by popular imagination. While the "play urge" is a subconscious entity in that its sudden manifestations often defy rational and commonly agreed explanation, play can portray and symbolize the whole spectrum of human emotions and life experiences. One could also add that play is the manifestation of a creative energy—an inherent psychological energy—that can burst forth in any circumstance or environment. That it was eminently present in the Holocaust, even if explaining its existence there is so elusive, should no longer be surprising or unexpected. The Holocaust, however, did more than alter the content and meaning of the play and games of the period; it also introduced new dimensions for play and the role of play. Indeed, it becomes immediately evident that in the wake of the Holocaust trauma, extraneous stimuli, and intrinsic urges, play and games went through an intense transformation and came to serve a purpose not normally attributed to them.

In order to understand this major deviation from the conventional, one must acknowledge three basic impulses that governed human behavior and conduct during the Holocaust: opposition to subjugation, adjustment to adversity, and the urge for survival. All three should be considered inherent, almost instinctual, in the human psyche. They were also closely interrelated, forming alternating stages of existence in a completely unconventional and irrational world. And, in that world, where the victims' responses to designs of extermination were strictly limited, the adults' creation of playgrounds and their organization of play activities and the children's own games served to formulate a defense mechanism.

Opposition, denoting a reaction against the subjugation of the mind and body, is a generic term. It encompasses a spectrum of human responses that run from defiance to armed resistance. The use of the term *opposition* instead of *resistance* is deliberate. It is vague enough to include comfortably the concept of play. The idea of "resistance" during the Holocaust has traditionally created mixed emotions and divergent opinions among historians and survivors alike. The question of what constitutes resistance, defiance, or other forms of opposition in general and their various degrees and manifestations is a difficult one. One would like to see a powerful resistance against an evil of such magnitude as the Holocaust; one wishes for heroic figures who stand with avenging swords in their hands and fallen enemies strewn at their feet. But whereas this has been the customary image of heroic resistance through history, this picture—connoting "armed resistance"—presents only one of many options of human reaction to annihilation. It restricts our understanding of a wide range of actions that can occur in opposing one's physical and mental oppression or demise. The essence of opposition, which includes resistance, defiance, and protest, encompasses more than armed action. The definition must include a wealth of human responses, especially when the means of and ability to respond are severely limited. A simple comment of the survivor Genia Silkes exemplifies well the problem of specifically defining resistance. An educator and one of the heroines of the Warsaw ghetto, she observed that "to live one more day is resistance. Amidst the dysentery and typhus, the starvation, is resistance. To teach and learn is resistance."[1]

Undoubtedly, Silkes's perception is more relevant to the general concept of survival than to conscious or deliberate resistance. Yet the ethos of *opposition* should accommodate many acts: fiercely willing oneself to outlive the oppressor; raising a clenched fist; pulling the trigger of a gun. Be that as it may, for a definition of opposition (defiance) it is imperative to transcend the conventional and rather narrow philosophical view of Holocaust historians.[2] Defiance is a psychological concept; it is a disposition, subconscious for the most part, to oppose one's annihilation by all possible means. In this light, the ultimate measure of heroism should not be whether it involves armed resistance. The measure should be whether it is able to overcome and oppose one's spiritual and physical subjugation. In the Holocaust this impulse toward defiance became just as integral to survival as food, warmth, and shelter, for it rekindled and sustained a spirit for survival. It also demonstrated the superiority of the victims over the persecutors who were unable to stop it or to respond to it.

If we accept this reasoning, then, the rationale behind the desperate efforts of the community to establish playgrounds and organizing play opportunities sounds more understandable. A community, clinging to dignity to its end, acted to reassert its freedom of choice. The mental and physical terror succeeded in destroying people physically, but it could not completely debase them morally. In Warsaw, Chaim Kaplan perceived this will to resist, to succeed against all odds. In describing the Hanukkah celebrations during the winter of 1940–41 he wrote with a sense of wonder about how "the enemy makes laws but they [Jews] don't obey them. . . . that is the secret of our survival. . . ." He exclaimed: "How much joy, how much of a feeling of national kinship there was in these Hanukkah parties! After sixteen months of Nazi occupation, we came to life again."[3]

It would not be inflating the concept of opposition to claim that children turned their play and games into a form of protest and a form of defiance, on both the subconscious and the conscious levels. Their activities reflected, unwittingly, the children's unique cognitive developmental levels and the confined context in which they took place. Hungry, battered, and terrorized, the children retained their humanness and their respect for life—their actions reaffirmed the primacy of existence by attempting to find equilibrium in an irrational world. Using play as a form of protest, deliberate opposition in essence, transcended the ordinary definition and understanding of heroism for it signified the ultimate spiritual resistance. Nazi decrees, for example, prevented an environment conducive to formal education. In fact, in many locales explicit prohibition of education was implemented, coinciding with the commencement of German occupation. The events of the perilous times proved that there are no limits for human ingenuity. Theresienstadt provides one glaring example of restrictive German policies and the Jewish attempts to circumvent them. The Youth Care organization of the camp (Jugendfuersorge) formed several "play groups" which replaced the formal school structure. A prisoner remembered after the war that "lessons had to be camouflaged as games." In the guise of play, genuine school subjects such as history, math, and geography were taught. Children took turns in alerting their classmates and teachers to the approach of SS men. On a moment's notice, children and teachers magically transformed the classroom into a play scene. Even the smallest details of these activities had to be well rehearsed, for if anyone were caught it could mean death for children and teachers alike.[4]

A teacher's reminiscences from Lublin indicate similar concerns and

14. "With beating hearts we conducted the lessons." A secret class in the Warsaw ghetto, 1941–42. Courtesy of the Ghetto Fighters' Museum, Israel.

problems. When German decrees forbade education in the ghetto, children in small groups gathered in a private apartment, smuggling with them scarce texts and notebooks:

> With beating hearts we conducted the lessons, simultaneously on the alert for the barking voices of the SS, who frequently raided Jewish homes. In such a case all incriminating traces immediately disappeared. Gone were the books and notebooks. The pupils began to play and the teacher became a customer: in a tailor's house he began to try on clothes and in a shoemaker's house—shoes.[5]

This form of play, like other games that will be mentioned later, can hardly classify as true manifestations of the "play urge," which should possess spontaneity and be void of tangible gains. This play existed as a deliberate ruse to cover something else. In general, there were many activities that were categorically forbidden yet were practiced nevertheless by the children. Kaplan's comment on dancing in the tormented ghetto offers one prominent example of an act of defiance. His words reveal a special intuition mixed with a large degree of optimism for the nuances of ghetto life. In an act of capriciousness, the German command forbade dancing, but the decree did not prevent the adult or youth populace from holding dances. The response was a tangible expression of the community's spiritual resistance to the enemy:

> There is a lot of frivolity in the ghetto, in order to somewhat lessen its sorrow. In the daytime, when the sun is shining, the ghetto groans. But at night everyone is dancing even though his stomach is empty. . . . It is almost a mitzvah to dance. The more one dances, the more it is a sign of his belief in the "eternity of Israel." Every dance is a protest against our oppressors.[6]

In analyzing this entry one might choose to dispute Kaplan's idealism or interpretation of this scene. Was the dancing indeed an act of defiance and "protest"; was it a conscious escape from reality, as he intimated elsewhere; or was it just wishful thinking on the part of the diarist? We have seen, again and again, that the greatest heroism, one that transcends the conventional meaning of the term, does not come from soldiers who are prepared for action and war. War carries with it a certain presumption of competition, some measure of equality in a contest where both sides can inflict pain and death. The Holocaust, however, was not a war and presented no balance. Indeed, a child's action offers a much more delicate heroism because it springs from inequality, powerlessness, and innocence and demonstrates the strength that can be derived from living by ideals that contradict the executioners' intended design.

In 1940 Kaplan described a situation in which the children of the ghetto disguised their scorn and ridicule toward a visiting potentate by exaggerating their "homage":

> Sometime our work is done by schoolchildren. The children of our poor, with whom the streets of Warsaw are filled at all hours of the day, are not afraid even of the despotic conquerors. . . . But these weeds watch every act of the conquerors and imitate the Nazis' manner of speech and their cruelty most successfully. For them this is nothing but good material for games and amusements. Childhood does much.
>
> Once there came into the ghetto a certain Nazi from a province where the Jews are required to greet every Nazi soldier they encountered, removing their hats as they do. There is no such practice in Warsaw, but the "honored guest" wanted to be strict and force the rules of his place of origin on us. A great uproar arose suddenly. . . . The little "wise guys," the true lords of the street, noticed what was going on and found great amusement in actually obeying the Nazi, and showing him great respect in a manner calculated to make a laughingstock

out of the "great Lord" in the eyes of all the passersby. They ran up to greet him a hundred and one times, taking off their hats in his honor. They gathered in great numbers, with an artificial look of awe on their faces, and would not stop taking off their hats. Some did this with straight faces, while their friends stood behind them and laughed. . . . That wasn't all. Riffraff gathered for the fun, and they all made noisy demonstration in honor of the Nazi with a resounding cheer.

This is Jewish revenge![7]

This scene conveys a fountain of baffling psychological complexities. It demonstrates that the children had a clear grasp of reality and the balance of power, but with deliberate cunning were able to retaliate by humiliating their humiliator. While the children possessed no obvious power of opposition, their gestures highlighted the absurdity of the German decrees and represented a subtle act of resistance. Without overestimating their accomplishment (after all, the Germans appear to have been oblivious to the motivating factors behind the children's behavior), the children's defiance presented a moral victory of a kind—a psychological boost for the oppressed. It was not an isolated phenomenon; it was just part of a burgeoning record of ghetto humor. Jews responded to German policies throughout the conquered territories with scorn wrapped in humor and jokes. Perhaps humor is not a clear instance of *resistance,* but rather belongs to the subgenre of *defiance* or *protest;* it was used to mediate stress and facilitated a psychological removal from the stress situation.

Defiance and protest are human reactions. They cannot rightfully be relegated only to the subconscious domain of human behavior for they can also be deliberate and purposeful acts that take many forms. "When the children learned," a teacher from the Lodz ghetto tearfully remembered, "that they were to be deported, a spontaneous fury seized them." They went to their garden and, in a burst of anger, trampled the few beds of beets. With the toes of their shoes they kicked every clod of earth and, in a rage of frustration, tore the plants out by their roots, throwing them all over the place.

"Nothing will grow after we have gone! Nothing will bloom in this garden!" a girl about ten years old screamed in rage.

"Nothing will grow! Nothing will bloom!" the others repeated and trod everything into the ground even more passionately.[8]

Although similar rage motivated the Westerbork children when the ill-fated train pulled in to take its usual human cargo toward the extermination centers in Poland, they responded with a studied silence instead of active rage. The inmates of the camp always greeted the train's arrival with a silent sorrow and scorn. For the children it was the legendary dragon, a Moloch who must be appeased with human sacrifices. Although the children had no guns, no knives, and no power—only boundless hatred toward this instrument of doom—they knew and felt the chill of Auschwitz, Treblinka, and Bergen Belsen in the air. The only recourse for protest available was to express their contempt. Mechanicus observed "a group of schoolchildren who were going to the moor and are in the habit of singing every day as they walk along went past the train in silence at the instigation of one of the children who cried out: 'Boys, there's the plague train again. Don't sing, do you hear!' "[9]

THIS SPIRIT OF protest and defiance became a conscious part of many ghetto games. Quite often it was hard even to recruit a group of children willing to play the hated enemy, the German soldiers. This was characteristic of all areas occupied by the Nazis. A child survivor, for example, remembered distinctly that in Gurs, in France, "nobody wanted to be German." In describing a war game among the ghetto children of Lodz, an observer noted that the children playing German soliders refused to sing the German song "We shall conquer the whole world." At the height of the great children's deportation of 1942, a small boy of nine stepped out and declared: "I don't want to be a German because the Germans take away little children from their mothers. . . . and they kill them!" And so the game immediately dissolved. The same source recorded the sequel: the children decided to play "deportation" with different children enacting the role of the grieving mother, the scared children, and the Germans. One of the organizers even instructed the participants: "The Germans will come to take you away, I won't let them, and you'll have to cry. . . ." And once more the same defiant boy stepped out of the group: "I don't want to be a German and I don't want to catch children."[10]

An additional factor that differentiates defiance from resistance is the degree of participation and involvement itself. While some acts of defiance were obviously purposeful and deliberate, they were carried out on a passive level. In fact many adult gestures of defiance and protest were enacted in the same manner. The first clear manifestation of symbolic resistance to German atrocities can be attributed to various forms of children's play. Through the magic world of make-believe children could express notions and desires that, though they existed among the adults, could not be voiced openly. In the Kovno ghetto, Lithuania, children used to play "gravedigging: they would dig a pit and would put a child inside and call him Hitler." In Vilna another popular game, even more elaborate and graphic than the former, was called "Liberation" or "Ponary." It enacted the tragedy of Vilna Jewry, which was decimated by Einsatzgruppen in the woods of

Ponary in 1941–42, but the game provided a curious twist for a poetic ending. In the simple words of a nine-year-old participant, which were recorded in 1946 immediately after the liberation, an intense drama was enacted:

> children playing "Jews" were led by the "Gestapomen" to Ponary, a wooded area in the Vilna district, to be killed. The "Jews," however, overpowered the "Gestapomen" and beat them with their own rifles [sticks]. The liberated "Jews" tied the hands of the "Gestapomen" with strings and took them to the place of execution instead of the "Jews." At their destination, they were lined up and with rifles [sticks] shot to death.[11]

Warlike games have always been a prominent and popular pastime of children everywhere. In times of war they understandably overshadow other play forms in their intensity and deliberateness. They offer a reflection of the feelings and loyalties of the youngsters involved. It should not come as a surprise, then, that in the games of the ghettos and camps the Jews and the Russians always won. Although my study has focused exclusively on Nazi-occupied Europe, it is relevant here to describe the experiences of the Jewish children who succeeded in escaping to the Soviet Union during the war. The children knew, as did their elders, the fate of the Jews in the occupied territories and they enacted it with frightful accuracy, until the endings, which always portrayed victory for the oppressed. Let the words of an eight-year-old speak for themselves:

> One time the "Germans" invaded our camp. This time Sanka was a "German" who was searching for "Jews." Because of my nose I was recognized as a "Jew" and was tortured to reveal the hiding places of other "Jews." Just then, my comrades to arm, we called them "the Tank-men," arrived, with raised hands. . . . We all, with the "Tank-men" encircled them [the Germans] and shouted "Hurrah!"[12]

COMPARING THE PLAY and games of the younger generation with the armed resistance of their elders is unnecessary. The children's activities did not alter the course of history or their immediate situation. Still, the "protest" that the children couched in their games belonged to the same genre of resistance behavior. It was not merely symbolic because through the games the children actively opposed, albeit on their own instinctual and cognitive levels, their mental subjugation and physical extermination. The notion of one's defiance and protest was also a part of a wider concept, "coping" in psychological terms, that formed a barrier against the painful intrusion of reality into the children's world, and at the same time created a bridge for accommodating this reality. This coping mechanism even could mobilize and channel a child's rage constructively, providing an "elation to be able to do something, not to be helpless."[13]

For psychologists investigating major traumas on the human psyche, the term *coping* connotes a "psychic numbing" that protects one "from reality too hard to face and too chaotic to formulate." This "coping" is a mechanism for dissociating oneself emotionally from the horrors around one. Presumably, then, one could, in time, "get used" to the nightmare of one's surroundings. That coping was often used as a defense against atrocity and as a means of surviving during the Holocaust is clear. It is also true that this general denial strategy was used more often and more effectively by adults, whose cognitive and rationalizing abilities were better developed than those of the children. Denial connoted a certain escape from reality—an escape that required a clear definition and assessment of reality.[14]

One can question whether coping with the atrocities of the Holocaust always exemplified a "psychic numbing"—at least in the case of the children. To cope with the acceptance of reality, play and games of children facilitated, often enough, psychic accommodation. In Auschwitz, children were seen to play with the limbs and fluttering hair of the dead as they were carted off in a pile to the crematorium. Auschwitz was obviously the ultimate experience in horror, but the bewildered words of Janusz Korczak reveal similar child behavior in Warsaw. We gain new meaning and perspective with this theory and exemplify, also, the gloom and desperation of a society in general and this humanist in particular. He observed in one of his excursions through the ghetto that

> a young boy, still alive or perhaps dead already is lying across the sidewalk. Right there three boys are playing horses and drivers; their reins have gotten entangled. They try every which way to disentangle them, they grow impatient, stumble over the boy lying on the ground. Finally one of them says:
>
> "Let's move on, he gets in our way."
>
> They move a few steps away and continue to struggle with the reins.[15]

Although these scenes undoubtedly demonstrate a form of coping, it is a coping that represents neither a "psychological removal" (the insulating of one's psyche from the surrounding trauma), nor a "denial" of reality. They exemplify the degree to which the children in the Warsaw ghetto had been brutalized, a degree that is extreme even in the skewed scale of the Holocaust. This discussion would not be complete without reiterating the obvious: these children played. This fact denies a "psychological removal" or a "psychic closing off"; exactly the opposite was taking place. The children exhibited a subconscious urge to assimilate existing realities and conscious efforts to learn to accommodate them. Older children understood the value of mentally removing themselves from a camp. Some in play and some in songs attempted to forget their situation. Thomas Geve, a young inmate in Birkenau, mentioned in his diary that "to us youngsters, the best way to dream ourselves away was to sing. We sang when penned up in our block during the many curfews, whilst having our weekly showerbath or out of loneliness."[16]

Younger children, however, comprehended and dealt with their convoluted world differently. Coping represented for them the understanding and management of an otherwise unbearable situation by resolving the disturbed balance of person-environment relationship directly or by diminishing the emotional distress resulting from it. A behavior directed to these aims exemplifies coping through mastering "a portion of the universe, external and internal." It involved a rationalization process on the level of a child. The Holocaust proved that the mind's power was almost omnipotent in assimilating atrocity and horror. A seven-year-old girl was "shaking from fright" upon entering the sewers of her hometown in search of shelter.

> I saw big, gray rats scurrying about; they ran by us like chickens. At the beginning I was terribly scared, but later I got used to it. Better to be with the rats than with the Germans—the rats do not know the difference between who is a Jew and who is not. But the Germans know how to kill all the Jews.[17]

Children's play was not only a simple reaction to the harrowing experiences they were living through; it was also a major force in shaping the ongoing stressful situation. Coping became a subconscious response of the mind to negotiate the requirements of novel and very confusing circumstances. In a world where unconventionality assumed a permanent dimension, every means, among them play, had to be harnessed to provide badly needed counterbalances to the crippling effects of reality. To overcome these effects was an especially acute problem in hiding. "The question of mental endurance," a young boy perceptively pondered, "was not less important than our physical resistance." This young boy described in graphic detail how his family hid for two years in a pit dug in a stable and covered with manure. The unbearable monotony, the fear of being discovered, the stench, and the danger of asphyxiation made life a veritable hell, ameliorated only by reading and chess.

The most important problem was to find some occupation. . . . The second occupation was chess. We played almost all day long creating interest not only for the players but also for the kibbitzers. To make the games more challenging, we played for stakes, for a potato or a spoonful of soup, food being the most precious of things to us. The losing side had to yield part of dinner, and we fought with bitter determination. . . .

Father . . . watched us play chess and specialized in stealing or rearranging pieces. This in turn brought about arguments and debates which killed time—a priceless gain. . . ."[18]

In the ecological setting of the Holocaust a strong affinity between coping and the concept of survival—the will to live by any means—seemed logical and indispensable. In fact, the relationship between play and Holocaust existence begins to make sense only when considered in conjunction with notions of survival—especially because the range of action at the disposal of both the leadership and the populace was so severely curtailed by German authorities. Behavior exhibited by children in a play setting was, then, eminently directed toward understanding their environment (assimilating) and learning to respond to its requirements. Their behavior was an arrangement of their needs and problems relating to the basic elements of life. Many of their games and play activities mirrored their overwhelming desire to stay alive. Kaplan's perceptive comment characterized this powerlessness: "The members of the ghetto, condemned to die, want to enjoy life as long as breath remains within them. But herein lies the trouble, for the people of the ghetto are limited in their ability to find the enjoyment they long for. Like the Nazis we utilize substitutes. You cannot imprison human desires."[19]

The children, who were in the most precarious position in the fight for survival, needed all the fortitude, perseverance, and inventiveness they could muster. And they "utilize[d] substitutes." Emmanuel Ringelblum of the Warsaw ghetto noted with amazement a street scene: "I saw a band of four or five children who eke out an existence playing in the street some child's game they have probably learned in school." This game enactment was not play in the true sense of the word but a form of "work" in the guise of play. The urge to harness all resources to remain alive was commmanded and reinforced by adults, by the wish of the condemned for the "sanctification of life"—tzu iberleybn. This Yiddish word, as was mentioned earlier, signified a will to survive, to remain alive, and to resist annihilation by all means available. An example of this spirit is given by Ringelblum, who in 1941 recorded seeing a beggar boy on the run-down streets of the ghetto singing "sweetly in Polish":

15. A child in the Warsaw ghetto, playing for bread. February 1941. Photo by Joe J. Heydecker, courtesy of Bildarchiv Preussische Kulturbesitz.

I'm not giving up my ration card,
There are better times a-coming.[20]

The song of the little beggar boy reflected the seemingly inexhaustible optimism and the overwhelming desire of the majority of ghetto children to outlast their tormentors. Kaplan's reference to the ghetto playgrounds shows this determination: "Nursery schools bring their infant charges to the parks, and older children have their lessons there. In short: an arrow in the Nazis' eyes! The arteries of life do not stop pulsing. We are schooled in life, skilled in the art of living." Perhaps Kaplan was too optimistic in his judgment of the ghetto's resolve, but a similar picture drawn by Kalmanowitch from Vilna independently seems to confirm Kaplan's perception. In his diary for 1942, Kalmanowitch comments upon the "life pulsating in the ghetto. . . . Children go to the woods with their teachers and adult men and women go along with them. Children play in the playground." Looking around, he recognized "tzu iberleybn" in spite of the destruction and death that reigned everywhere. In a nursery where mothers left their children from seven in the morning to six in the evening, 150 toddlers and young children could still smile. He exclaimed: "In ghetto circumstances the order is remarkable. . . . what a vitality in this people on the brink of destruction!"

A further comment from Kaplan gives depth to the picture. Seeing the increasingly threatening clouds, Kaplan had a positive thought even in the darkest hour: "In general, laughter is still evident. The youth goes on as always, busy with sports even when they are hungry." Then he added with a touch of defiance:

> A nation that can live in such terrible circumstances as these without losing its mind, without committing suicide—and which can still laugh—is sure of survival. Which will disappear first, Nazism or Judaism?
>
> I am willing to bet! Nazism will go first![21]

The children's psychological and physical adaptability seems remarkable in light of the extreme conditions they were subjected to. In the Plaszow camp, where the commandant deceitfully collected the children under the guise of a child-care facility, children bounced back from their dismal state within a few weeks. They were washed, fed, and allowed to "run around in the playground in front of the club. . . . They were children again." Similar transformation took hold of the children from the Bialystok ghetto. Their tragic tale is one of the most illuminating examples of the resiliency and will for life of ghetto children. One thousand two hundred and sixty Jewish children from that ghetto were transferred to the Theresienstadt camp after witnessing the execution of their parents and older brothers and sisters. They were to be exchanged, according to some nebulous Nazi plans, for Germans interned by the Allies. A contemporary described these children: "They were terrified and appeared to be dumb; many were bare-footed, all in pitiful rags and half-starved. With their tiny hands they clasped little boxes or prayer books, if they had anything to clasp at all."[22]

These little children had gone through everything and knew everything. They were familiar with the reputation of "bath houses" that were really gas chambers. An eyewitness account reported what happened when the Germans attempted to push them into the showers for a genuine bath: "The despairing children clung to each other, weeping and embracing one another amidst the crying." Because the Germans expected to exchange these and five thousand other Jewish children from Lodz for Germans in Allied hands, the children were treated relatively decently and their conditions underwent a radical change following their ordeal in Bialystok. During their six weeks in Theresienstadt, the group was given double food rations, decent shoes, and clothing. The other children at Theresienstadt reached out and helped their unfortunate contemporaries. A brief diary note of a little Czech boy from the camp mentioned that "1,500 children will arrive tonight. They are from Poland. We are making toys and little bags and nets for them, etc." In a later entry, the same boy recorded his impressions of the new prisoners with the sharp eye and honesty of a child: "They look awful. You can't guess how old they are, they all have old, strained faces and tiny bodies. . . . They all have such frightened eyes."[23]

The new children got accustomed to their environment quickly. Although a strict segregation between them and their fellow children prisoners was in force, the compassionate gifts of little toys reached them. The camp witnessed the power of "tzu iberleybn." In spite of their harrowing experiences, these children's natural vitality reasserted itself and they relaxed, sang children's songs, and began to play games. There are no records of the nature or content of their games. Maybe the children responded to the goodness of their helpers by reverting to innocent play and rhymes of a happier time. Maybe they were forced by subconscious urges to enact their more recent and tragic past in play form, as the Auschwitz children did. But the laughter of young voices was heard again. The cruel sequel to this story, one so familiar in the Holocaust, was that these children and the fifty-three volunteer nurses recruited from among the camp inmates never reached a neutral country. After six weeks they were shipped to the gas chambers of Auschwitz.

THE POWERS OF adaptation and survival were closely connected with the children's ability to enact atrocities and thus facilitate a process of accommodation to the almost unbearable reality. While this process will be described further, it might be noted that an adjustment manifested itself not only in a content transformation of traditional activities but also in the invention of games suited specifically for Holocaust environment and, consequently, survival. These activities were an amalgamation of instinctual stimuli and conscious drives to control and manage the person-environment relationship. It seems evident that the children's behavior in play articulated skills necessary for survival. The previously mentioned game in the Lodz ghetto in which little girls enacted the hardship of their mothers trying to secure food on ghetto coupons is a good example of preparing for and socializing a child into future roles and life experiences which might ensure survival.

Additional support for this notion can be gained from one of the most popular games of the ghetto children in Vilna. The game was called "building a bunker." Even youngsters of relatively tender age diligently ran across the yards, collecting bricks and planks. The digging and constructing was time-consuming and hard, but the children played the game feverishly and relentlessly. The earnestness of the little builders later caused much trouble for the adult population. The play "bunkers" were so real that German raiders mistook them for real ones and were more thorough in searching the area. One participant in the building endeavors recalled immediately after the war that "they [Germans] made a general search and actually in this courtyard found several bunkers with 30 men." One wonders whether the building activity was a conscious effort on the part of the children or was instinctual. This and similar descriptions of authentic ghetto games point to the latter. Although the wholesale building of hiding places (called "malines") by adults provided the obvious example for this play experience, the children's zeal points to a subconscious motivation to find shelter.[24]

One Holocaust survivor recently remarked that the hopes for survival never had any logical foundation. No one was guaranteed survival. Irrationality entered into every aspect of life and death. These were times "when a man ought to be more afraid of living than of dying," as a philosopher remarked, and the conscious mind had to play a most important part in one's quest for survival. The children's consciousness, however, reflected their cognitive level. It was mentioned previously that children studied and lessons were conducted under the guise of a game or play. A survivor of the Riga ghetto noticed inadvertently how ghetto children camouflaged other illegal activities with innocent games. As background for this, it is important to know that the ghetto's Kommandant Krause executed anyone, regardless of age or gender, who as much as smuggled a loaf of bread into the ghetto. In this incident, the children came with their kindergarten teachers to play in the close proximity of the ghetto fence. They innocently threw a ball or sang "ring-around-the-rosy." When their parents returned in the afternoon from their labor details outside the ghetto, the children ran to the fence to "take the provisions smuggled in by their parents and disappear as fast as their little legs [would] carry them."[25] Was their activity play in the truest sense of the word? It could not have been. The fact that parents faced death when caught, and often in front of their children, should be enough to support this unequivocal answer.

The way in which chess saved the life of a fourteen-year-old boy is perhaps instructive of the role the "conscious" can play. The backdrop is Bergen Belsen of 1944, which was writhing in the agony of hunger and typhoid. The commandant of the camp, SS Hauptsturmfuehrer Josef Kramer (who became known as the "Beast of Belsen") withheld the bread ration of the entire camp for three days in punishment for an attempt to get a letter out. This decree was tantamount to the death penalty for many of the emaciated inmates.

> I tried to figure out how to get through the next few days. What could I do to get my mind off food? Then I got the idea; there was a fellow in my barrack who had a chess set. I went over to him and asked him

> if he wanted to sell it to me. Of course, I couldn't buy it with money; there wasn't any, and money was useless here. I managed to talk him into selling me his chess set for two rations of bread, which meant that I wasn't to get bread for FIVE WHOLE DAYS. I had my reasons. I took the set to my bunk, and for the next three days I did nothing but play chess with my friend, Walter. We concentrated on the game so intensely that we forgot all about our hunger, so the days went by quickly.[26]

It is necessary to resort again to some theoretical reasoning, even if it can provide only partial answers, in explaining the use of play for the very specific purpose of survival. No one can explain this notion with a single theory of behavior and certainly no one can formulate a single theory about the function of play in this behavior. One thing, however, is evident: the eminent play theorist Huizinga's concept and rationale of play is almost useless in explaining the occurrence of play or play behavior in the Holocaust. In Huizinga's theories, just as in the popular imagination, play assumes mythical qualities of innocence, purity, and removal from everyday life. In most instances, however, play was neither free, frolicsome, nor beyond the ordinary. In recalling play activities in the Riga ghetto, a survivor readily agreed that children played games reflective of their environment (i.e., Aktion, Kontrolle) but they always played them in the back of the houses where the inquisitive eyes of the German sentries could not see the game. Their caution sprang from an awareness that their activities might provide ideas for the brutal guards to enact in real life.[27]

Although long neglected, one of the classical theories of play by Karl Groos might be applicable to explain children's play as an agent for survival. He argued, at the turn of the century, that children's play was not only not divorced from reality, but, in fact, that the behavior involved in play articulated skills necessary for survival. One cannot deny that playing certain games created situations for ghetto and camp children that inculcated skills for life's continuation. Groos's theory, although it received strong support through the years from anthropologists, was intended for an environment bound by rational and humane conditions. It falls understandably short of providing a viable theory for either the nature of play or the phenomenon itself in the Holocaust. His view that children's play behavior is governed by fundamentally subconscious impulses propelling them to play in itself would not stand up to the realities of the Holocaust. In that situation forms of play assumed a more and more utilitarian hue, turning into forms of work while losing their spontaneity, playfulness, and innocence.

The Holocaust experience involved such complexity that conscious perseverance and human imagination had to be severely taxed if one was to survive. Nothing can replicate the Holocaust, but laboratory studies of play demonstrated that play behavior of children is dependent on the play setting. The ghettos, camps, and horrid hiding places constituted the setting of an obviously much more realistic "experiment." In examining these conditions, it seems obvious that environmental factors became major determinants of formulating play practices and behavior. Both play practices and behavior were learned responses to the constellation of contingencies inherent in the abysmal conditions and life-threatening situations that surrounded the children. Play proved to be an eminently suitable means for appraising, assimilating, and mediating these contingencies. A survivor remembered the experience of being hidden under a hospital table, seeing "just legs walking back and forth for hours at a time" without being able to move or make a sound. "I would just want to scream and go crazy. It was very boring and I had a very good imagination. I believe it's crucial to surviving, your imagination. I would make up all kinds of stories, imaginary things."[28] Looking beyond the external, we must also consider a subconscious drive, a constant striving on the part of the human organism to reestablish an equilibrium in an utterly irrational and unpredictable universe. Techniques of opposition, coping, and survival were reflected in children's play—not unexpectedly—for play practices and behavior became compensatory agents in relieving stress and providing a process for accommodating the painful and traumatic existence of that time.

6
They Play before They Die

"But these children are not playing—they only make-believe it is play"

PLAY IS FUNDAMENTAL for life—a deliberate and purposeful act—and play in a given society must reflect society itself. As a cultural and psychological phenomenon it can neither isolate nor insulate itself or the participant from broader social events. Simultaneously, a playground must accommodate itself and its culture to the rules and themes embodied in the broader culture of the society. "The concentration camps," a Hungarian inmate in Auschwitz conjectured philosophically, "have created a civilization within a civilization. And in this new civilization the truths and laws whose validity we believed in for centuries have been turned upside down."[1] In studies of this milieu, discussions about the origin and source of play and play forms must transcend the conventional arguments of social scientists' theories and hypotheses. Just like the evil of the Holocaust, the motivation of play of the children who were victims of this evil challenges the imagination. Although we must ignore completely a romanticized notion of innocence as a means of explanation, we are hard put to come up with an adequate answer for how and why—and against all odds—a flickering flame of humanity could survive in the guise of children's play.

Diaries and memoirs establish the fact that children and adults played during this period. Previous chapters have dealt with the function of these play activities in a coping process that facilitated survival. The hauntingly recurring questions of why and how play was at all possible, however, could be answered only through an exhaustive search for and an examination and synthesis of psychological and anthropological theories about human behavior.[2] It must be reiterated that at face value the establishment of playgrounds and the organization of play activities seemed almost delusional, irrational, and highly abstract acts in light of the surrealistic, otherworldly backdrop of human misery. Yet these steps were not incidental expressions of a tormented and hunted society and culture. In attempting to find some explanation for these actions, some recent studies on the influence of children on the psycho-physiological state of adult groups provide some revealing insight. Results from laboratory experiments show that crying babies elicited much higher levels of anxiety and distress from adults than smiling children. The creation of the playgrounds and play opportunities by adult society should be seen as having been motivated by a strong desire to "bathe our children in laughter" and to provide, thereby, a spiritual uplift for the adult population. Mary Berg was only sixteen when she was keeping a diary of the Warsaw ghetto. In spite of her youth, she presented many perceptive observations about the physical and mental agony of the ghetto. She felt in 1942 that "the smiling rosy faces of the children were perhaps the best reward of those who had created this little refuge [playground] for the little prisoners of the ghetto."[3]

The motivation for the establishment of playgrounds in ghettos and camps was part of an active and conscious search for normalcy amid the social, psychological, and cultural dislocations of a deeply traumatized society. That in retrospect normalcy was only a myth should not detract from the sincerity of these efforts. The significance of myths is not that they are based on truth but that we believe in them, that they propel us into action and provide ideals to live by. Ghetto and camp culture was a derivation of wider sociopsychological undercurrents imposed mainly by the new conditions. The interaction of this drastically altered environment with traditional values and cultural norms gave a new form and content to life. The playgrounds represented desperate attempts to regain a sense of balance, an equilibrium in both the spiritual and the physical realms, for the adults as much as for the children. For the adults it provided a sense of regained mastery of their own fate, a free will for "self-determination."

The Jewish leadership had been propelled by other more subconscious forces to create a sheltering mechanism. Their urge was to regain a basic freedom of human thought. Considering the utterly limited means for the expression of any autonomy, in retrospect, we can see that these efforts had additional ramifications. By providing "shelter" and "protection" for the traumatized children, adult society also indirectly obtained an important, albeit faint, promise for the future—the promise for the survival of the next generation and the whole race.

This picture can be further sketched in by mentioning the almost atavistic impulse of every civilization to bestow upon future generations a legacy by which to be remembered. Besides spiritual reminders there also should be physical markers (e.g., the pyramids of the ancients) that show generations to come that people have lived here. There is an eerie premonition in the words of a Jewish official in the Vilna ghetto, Joseph Muszkat, at the opening of a newly built sports- and playground: "If one, in the future, would like to discover traces of our life in the ghetto, and there would be no documents or diaries to be found to bear witness, this site will be a genuine symbol of an unrestrainable vitality and an unrelenting will for survival in us. . . ."[4]

ALTHOUGH PEOPLE SPOKE of the future, it was murky—full of uncertainties and ambiguities. The adult society built and established playgrounds and parks primarily to shelter mentally and to preserve physically the future generation, and in return this effort uplifted, if only for a moment, the morale of the community. But was there any justification for the adult society's belief that play could function as a sheltering mechanism? Were the adults' valiant efforts successful in transforming the lives and future of the children or were they only a futile gasp for air by a suffocating community? It is difficult to dissociate oneself emotionally in answering these questions. After all, the ultimate sources for information on the success of the playgrounds as a psychological shelter would be the children themselves, and only a precious few lived through the ordeal. In spite of the executioners' pedantic efforts to erase all traces of their crime, however, these sources left an array of diaries, documents, and notes, that illuminate the children's anguish and their yearnings for a better life and a better future.

These yellowed and crumpled pages are radiantly honest, complementing well the tormented memories of survivors. They convey a profound difference between the role and function assigned to play and games by ghetto society and their actual effectiveness in blocking out painful reality. The discrepancy should not come as a surprise because history taught us, through the words of the philosopher, that "there are times when a man ought to be more afraid of living than of dying." The words of a little girl from the Warsaw ghetto condensed this unequal struggle into a sharply etched description of this duality.

> When I am in play, I forget my hunger. I forget that outside are such evil Germans even existing. Early in the morning I rush to the child care center and I wish that the day would never end, because when it is getting dark, we all have to return home. In my room it is so full with dark shadows and black fear.[5]

It was a battle for life and as in all battles there were little triumphs. On balance, however, the children lost the war for survival because the engulfing shadows of the surrounding depravity were too powerful to allow the protective rays of play to shelter the young. Rare moments of joy were not able to outweigh the misery. A chronic crisis of powerlessness of ghetto administrations and, more so, of concentration camp inmates coupled with pervasive financial incapacity rendered even the most sincere efforts to protect or save the children marginal. The games and play opportunities provided little relief from physical misery and were insufficient shelter for the long range as well. Hunger and suffering destroyed the body and occupied the mind, but the uncertainty and precariousness of existence shackled the spirit. The children were never allowed to forget the transports leaving regularly eastward into nothingness. The prose of a fifteen-year-old from Theresienstadt who died in Auschwitz revealed the collective fear: "from time to time, one thousand unhappy souls would come here and . . . from time to time, another thousand unhappy souls go away." In Theresienstadt there was at least a semblance of orderliness and a little hope. In the gruesome existence of the Warsaw ghetto it seemed almost delusional to assume that creating play settings, as a quasi refuge, had any power to insulate the children from reality for any length of time. They were not able to erase the knowledge of a sinister future looming several blocks away. The Umschlagplatz (collection point for Warsaw Jews to be deported to death camps) was in close proximity to the playgrounds and courtyards where toddlers played in the sandbox. The frightening swiftness with which play and deportation alternated in the lives of the young ones can only magnify the inability of play to shelter them.

Janina David was the daughter of a ghetto policeman who, because of her father's status, was relatively immune from deportation. Her playmates, however, were not. As an unofficial supervisor of the children in her courtyard, she described vividly the sudden change from serenity to fright and the resulting agony of children and mothers:

> When the raid started I was downstairs with them, watching the toddlers in the sand-pit we had built that summer.
>
> Suddenly there were shrill whistles in the street, panicky feet rushed past and the gate was slammed. We heard the lorries pulling up outside the house and commands shouted in German and Polish. In a moment the courtyard was empty. I was almost on our staircase when I saw one of our neighbors, a young woman, shrieking on her balcony and tearing her hair. She was on the second floor and her children, a baby of six months and a two-year-old girl, were still in the

> sand-pit. Without thinking I turned back, flew across the courtyard, grabbed the baby and, with the terrified toddler clutching my skirt, reached the stairs just as the front gate was opening and the "action squadron" marched in.[6]

Similarly, in the unpredictable moment-to-moment existence of concentration camps, play and sports adjusted, like every other facet of life, to the surrounding uncertainty. "The chess contest has broken down completely and been forgotten," Philip Mechanicus, the Dutch chronicler of Westerbork, recorded laconically, "firstly because people taking part had to go on the transports and secondly because people's minds were very much taken up with the cancellation of exemptions and the results of this as far as deportation was concerned."[7]

The fear is almost palpable through the pages of the extant diaries. They show that there was no complete escape from misery, suffering, and, above all, fear. For children and adults alike the backdrop for all life activities was the dreaded "train for the transport," which left punctually toward Auschwitz, Treblinka, and Chelmno. For Mechanicus in Westerbork, just like for many others elsewhere, there was "always sorrow in the background." In Westerbork it was the sorrow resulting from the separation of families and an intuitive fear of the unknown, for no one knew exactly the real meaning of Auschwitz, Treblinka, and other extermination camps. In the Riga ghetto the sense of doom was much more keen. Josef Katz, who was a young strapping fellow and an athlete before the war, resignedly noted in his diary that "there are gaps among the [soccer] players—people who were sent to an Aussenkommando [labor detail] or shot during the past week." Yet the games went on, just as the tormented life went on. The only change was the face of a new player; the games between the Latvian and German Jewish police continued "on the same Tin Square where the gallows stood."[8]

Fear had the power to assert its presence in the subconscious mind of every child. Mechanicus's words, resonating with shock and sorrow reflected the common helplessness and despair felt by the adult population in attempting to shelter the young from the surrounding world: "In the night the little daughter of friends of mine dreamt that her doll had to go on the transport." Even the children of the so-called privileged individuals (members of the ghetto police or administration) were not immune from immediate capture and deportation. Fear was omnipresent: "While I sat over my solitaire [cards] my ears were straining to catch the slightest sound of approaching footsteps, or a voice, or a policeman's whistle. And always at the back of my mind was the question of what I would do if They came."[9] A child was never able to forget the ever-present dangers of the absurd world in which he or she had to survive. When one passed as an Aryan, using false identity, any mistake was tantamount to death. One's guard had to be up at all times. Every young child knew the rules of this game—the game of survival. An eight-year-old boy, for example, was perfectly aware of the calamity it would be for himself and his parents if he were to go swimming: "I could play freely with the children but when my friends called me to go swimming with them, I made myself sick so that they could not recognize that I was a Jew. Because when one bathed one had to undress completely. My mother warned me that I should never show myself naked for anyone."[10]

Jewish society's efforts to rescue the ghetto and camp children from moral and mental turpitude did not alter fundamentally their situation. One of the most tragic echoes of the Holocaust was adult society's acute concern and despair about the moral deterioration of the youth. Stanislaw Adler, who was an official of the Jewish Police, summed up the problem of the youth: "Spending the whole day in the street, the child has the opportunity to observe everything that society usually hides in shame, and bad examples find very fertile ground in the mind of a child for all kinds of influences." He also recorded seeing Adam Czerniakow of Warsaw wringing "his hands in despair: 'Children are our future, what will become of them?' " There was also the troubling question of what impression the future generation, if it survived, would make on the world. That an advanced stage of moral and physical decay was perceived to have set in can be deduced from an observer's pessimistically frank question about the youths from Lodz "those 'natural jewels' of the ghetto kingdom—the 'coalminers.' . . . what a degenerated, mutilated, and deformed generation will have to come from this ghetto society. . . . in seeing them [the new generation] what will the enemies and haters of the Jews say . . . ?"[11]

THE GHETTOS AND camps stamped an indelible mark on the psyche and behavior of the youth. Many children grew up prematurely—at least mentally—but they often regressed psychologically to an infantile stage. On the one hand, a child of the ghetto, even at a tender age, knew the meaning of Ponary, and what happened there. The children were playing "Action," "Breaking into Hiding Places," "Massacre in Ponary," "Returning the Clothing of the Dead." On the other hand, and almost parallel to this intelligent awareness, was a marked deterioration that took place on an emotional level. A survivor of Westerbork and Theresienstadt mentioned that she refused to play in the sandbox at Westerbork because it was "dirty." In explaining her refusal she noted that "children regressed to infant habits in the camp and they regressed also in the sense of soiling their pants. They did not seem to care about it and laughed about it as they did this in the sandbox."[12]

Although parental and educational values still influenced, however faintly, the moral fabric of child society, the psychological brutalization of the young generation assumed many forms. The content of children's games was one of the most obvious manifestations of the combination of pre-Holocaust values and the drastically altered environment. Children from middle-class sociocultural backgrounds engaged in play behavior that baffled their elders because it transcended completely accepted societal norms in both their pre- or post-Holocaust cultures. Mechanicus noticed with consternation that a "number of small children are playing on sewage pipes. They are discussing, as a perfectly ordinary topic of conversation, how many fleas each of them caught last night." Gabriele Silten speaks of a similar recreation and, in retrospect, with similar shock. When she was incarcerated in Theresienstadt the morning ritual included a competition with her friend for who could catch and kill more fleas and bedbugs. "It was more challenging to catch the fleas," she recalled, "because they jump, whereas the bedbugs don't; they just crawl and are therefore easy to catch."[13] In comparison with other ghetto games one might view this behavior as a mild form of aberration from the norm. An infinitely more shocking game the children played was "Returning the Clothing of the Dead," which was an enactment of the killing of the Vilna Jews in Ponary. Before their execution, the victims had been forced to undress—and a small portion of their clothing was returned to the ghetto by the executioners. Children played out this whole drama with chilling accuracy.

The frequency and banality of death and society's acceptance of it made an everlasting impression on the children's psyche. Because it became so common, death assumed a grotesque, almost surrealistic dimension in which corpses became mere objects belonging to the streets just like cobblestones and garbage. Janina David, the young girl from Warsaw whom I have quoted before, wrote that "I looked at them all with wide eyes and my mind shut. I refused to think of what I was seeing, and even more resolutely I forbade myself to feel. I stepped over the naked skeletons and looked at them with careful indifference. They were a race apart." An unemotional acceptance of death by children was evident also in many other ghettos and camps. Reflecting the despair of adult society about the mental and psychological callousness of the young, the historian Ringelblum noted that "death lies in every street. The children are no longer afraid of death. In one courtyard, the children played a game tickling a corpse."[14]

The children's play behavior was not the rejection of reality; it was reality itself. As Tadeusz Borowski wrote about Auschwitz (where there was even a swimming pool and a soccer field): "Between two throw-ins in a soccer game, right behind my back, three thousand people had been put to

16. The funeral cart served several purposes—it carried the dead, transported food, and was a toy for the children. Water color by Helga Weissowa-Hoskova. Courtesy of Precious Legacy Project, Linda Altschuler, B'nai B'rith Klutznik Museum, Washington, D.C.

death."[15] A deep and profound gulf separated the role and function that adult society saw for play and games and what they actually accomplished in the Holocaust. They had no complete power to insulate the children from reality, and they could not erase the knowledge of the inevitable doom. There were constant reminders, reinforced endlessly, that death was an integral part of the life cycle. Paintings show that in Theresienstadt when the funeral hearse was not carrying heaps of corpses to the mass graves, the children played with it, inventing many games for its use. One of the most gripping paintings of the same theme is by Norbert Troller. The picture portrays the courtyard of the Dresden Barracks where a funeral, a soccer match, bread distribution, and gymnastics for young girls are being conducted simultaneously—a symbolic life cycle in a concentration camp.

In the final account, one must concede that the actual or purported efforts to create a sane, sheltered, and rational world for the children were short-lived at best. "With great sacrifice," a Jewish labor leader resignedly admitted, "we managed to perform pathetic wonders." During the deportation of children from the Lodz ghetto, a teacher remembered a child, Ettie, only five years old, who took with her on her voyage into eternity "an innocent smile" and "her soft baby doll on whose dress" her sister "had stitched two yellow stars."[16] This shows, as poignantly as any other example, that in spite of all attempts no playgrounds or other humanitarian endeavors could either arrest the rapidly deteriorating situation of the children or change the well-designed course of destruction. That is not to say that a community, geared for emergency, did not gain some psychological benefits. But, given the backdrop of cold, starvation, and death, playgrounds or play activities could provide only a temporary refuge. The spirit cannot rise when the body has sunk too low. Jan Karski, a representative of the Polish government in exile, himself not a Jew, was smuggled into the Warsaw ghetto to see conditions and report to his superiors in London. "Everywhere there was hunger, misery, the atrocious stench of decomposing bodies, the pitiful moans of dying children" he noted in his report.

> We passed a miserable replica of a park—a little square of comparatively clear ground in which a half-dozen nearly leafless trees and a patch of grass had somehow managed to survive. It was fearfully crowded. Mothers huddled close together on benches nursing withered infants. Children, every bone in their skeletons showing through their taut skins, played in heaps and swarms.
>
> "They play before they die," I heard my companion on the left say, his voice breaking with emotion.
>
> Without thinking—the words escaping even before the thought had crystallized—I said:
>
> "But these children are not playing—they only make-believe it is play."[17]

The constantly recurring question of whether the adult community could have done anything more, given its chronic powerlessness, justifiably crosses one's mind, but a negative answer must be almost automatic. After all, the unmasked reality decreed that play activities could make, at best, the adjustment to that life somewhat less painful; it was not possible to postpone its inevitable end. Indeed, a fundamental transformation took place not only in the form but also in the nature of the play activities, for they came to resemble reality more and more. A survivor of the Kovno ghetto, Dr. Aaron Peretz, has described the effect that the executions had on the children and the games they played:

> The children in the ghetto would play and laugh, and in their games the entire tragedy was reflected. They would play grave-digging: they would dig a pit and would put a child inside and call him Hitler. And they would play at being gatekeepers of the ghetto. Some of the chil-

> dren played the parts of the Germans, some of Jews, and the Germans were angry and would beat the other children who were Jews. And they used to play funerals. . . .
>
> The Jewish child was prematurely grown up. We were amazed to observe how children three or four years old understood the tragedy of the situation, how they clammed up when it was necessary, how they knew when to hide. We ourselves could not trust our ears when we heard small children, offered a sedative, say: "Doctor, this is not necessary, I shall be quiet, I shall not scream."[18]

The ability to escape reality through play, under these circumstances, could not have been more than a myth. But it was a beautiful myth—it created moral ambiguity showing things as one might think they ought to be, not as they were. Thus the adult inmates of camps and ghettos gained a certain buffer by denying reality—at least for a brief spell. I, again, quote from Kaplan's rich legacy of careful observations: "Man's nature is such," he wrote in January of 1942, "that in times of crisis the urge to 'eat, drink, and be merry' is more powerful. Such people, feeling they 'may as well be hanged for a sheep as for a lamb,' are in constant pursuit of pleasure."[19] It is almost certain that no similar sentiments were attached to children's play. Here lies a noticeable gulf that sets apart children's responses to mental trauma from those of the adults.

In earlier chapters I have implied that a distinct difference existed between adults' and children's play in the Holocaust. I was deliberately vague because very little has been done to establish general dividing lines between these two concepts in past play research or literature. Yet one can postulate with some certainty that the two obviously differ. Although some would argue about whether adults played in the Holocaust, evidence shows that it was a common response in many instances. An "escape mechanism" used by adults in times of trauma and horror is indeed immersing oneself in feverish activity—especially anything that creates a temporary shelter removed completely, or as much as possible, from the existing reality. The psychologist Bruno Bettelheim, who himself experienced the horrors of a concentration camp, emphasized that a "feeling of detachment, by rejecting the reality of the situation in which the prisoners found themselves, might be considered a mechanism safeguarding the integrity of their personalities." One often finds what appears to be a hedonistic attitude among the adult population in ghettos and camps. "Only the dances kept on with a more feverish undercurrent," wrote a ghetto dweller from Riga who talked of the "hectic straining that expressed a preoccupation with the few pleasures the ghetto could offer, a frantic wish to live fast and dangerously before the end came."[20] Sexual promiscuity described by many ghetto observers also served as an escape mechanism.

Basing her argument on Freud and Erikson, Veronica Axline alluded to this use of play as a mechanism that encourages individuals to divest themselves of negative experiences by handing them on, by purging them, or by transferring them—processes whereby they are adapting to, or assimilating new conditions and situations.[21] As was already noted, these were forms of coping or of effecting a "psychic numbing" for adult society. Without inflating this concept, however, children's play has a dignity of its own. The games of the young facilitated a potential for "coping" on a different level. Play could never fulfill the function of an "escape mechanism" in the traditional sense of offering an escape from conditions beyond one's control—as contemporary accounts intimated it did for adult society. Children's games and play neither transcended reality nor changed it. They faithfully reflected it, becoming an integral part of it, or at least of what children thought reality to be. The difference, then, can be attributed in a large part also to the differences between the cognitive and rationalizing power of an adult and a child. When family members of two generations were allowed to stay together, the children possessed a greater ability to negotiate the novel demands of ghetto existence than did their parents, whose constant humiliation destroyed both self-esteem and the will to resist. Adults were anchored in the past too strongly to accommodate themselves to the intricacies of existence in the Holocaust. They formed a new value system with difficulty and never without confrontation with the past. Their only way out was to escape from their forlorn reality. Children, on the other hand, possessed a chameleonlike adaptability. They were able to assimilate change quickly and adapt readily to new conditions.

That play had a unique role in this "assimilation" and "accommodation" process seems certain. Play under ordinary conditions has elicited much discussion and speculation among scientists or casual observers. What is it? How should it be defined? What is its function? The last question is perhaps the most intriguing to Western minds that are often trained to understand the world in utilitarian terms. The exact function of play in "normal" societies may never be concluded; in the Holocaust culture, however, it did serve to make growing youngsters familiar with their environment. It is beyond argument that it helped in the children's quest for understanding their chaotically irrational universe, providing a sort of "enculturation" process. The content and format of the games children engaged in were able to provide the children with a "buffered" experience within which they could learn about their surroundings and the adaptive skills needed to respond to them. One single theory, again, would be inadequate to present an explanation of how this process took place and from where its motivation sprang. Beyond that, in their explanations of human play no play theorists have ever adequately conceived contingencies that might explain the period of the Holocaust. One must also proceed from the presupposition, ignored by some of the theorists, that play urge, play content, and play behavior in themselves are highly distinct concepts. The first is the expression of an innate and creative energy of an organism to engage in an activity while the latter two combine environmental stimuli and personality characteristics to enact this activity.

One firmly anchored belief of popular culture is that children's play is "anti-serious." Of course, the role that play occupies in human lives is infinitely complex. If we accept the theory that play, consciously or subconsciously, had distinct functions in the lives of the children, the axiom that play in the Holocaust was not only part of the "seriousness" but was also the "serious" reality itself must gain credibility as well. In establishing, however, the rationale and causality of their play urge and play behavior, most of the conventional psychological and social theories seem to hold little relevance or power.[22]

Among the often quoted and argued about theories in play research, Johan Huizinga's ideas on play contribute very little in the way of adequate explanation of children's play in the particular milieu of the Holocaust. Huizinga proposed a highly romanticized philosophical view of a free, out of the ordinary, and frolicsome child's world—a world that cannot exist at any time and certainly did not in the Holocaust. Other classical theories, with the exception perhaps of those of Groos, are equally empty of explanation. As was discussed in the previous chapter, Groos advanced the axiom of a functional interpretation of play in which children's play articulates skills necessary for survival. Although his ideas reflected a strong influence of the turn-of-the-century philosophical trends, these ideas could not be equated with an instinct of the survival of the species, in a Darwinian context. Rather, I have shown that in the Holocaust a strong tendency prevailed on the part of the children to engage in play activities, both imaginary play and enacting atrocities, through which they were able to learn adaptive techniques for their world.[23]

In searching for answers to "Why do children play?" or to whether an inherent play urge exists at all, one is compelled to look toward some of the recent theories that attempt to understand the roots of play from physiological, ecological, and cognitive perspectives. One complex and widely promulgated interpretation of the play urge assumes that a stimulus-seeking drive for "arousal" exists within both man and animal. In simple terms, the organism has a need to avoid boredom, a need that reflects the nervous system's state of perpetual activity. A normal organism needs constant sensory input, i.e., arousal, from the environment (hence the name "arousal theory") in order to satisfy its need for stimulation.[24] Corresponding research aligned this theory with neurological studies, which indeed supported the idea that the need for arousal is both a physiologically and a mentally directed motivational drive. While one must exercise caution in transferring results of animal experiments to human situation, recent animal studies revealed that brief periods of hunger or discomfort by themselves do not inhibit play and game; in fact, exactly the opposite proved to be the case. These experiments showed that hunger and discomfort among animals induce a marked increase in the amount and intensity of play and play behavior.[25] Moreover, the combination of stressful situations and initial hunger propelled an even more intense and heated play and should be considered as important facilitators of arousal. This finding is reminiscent of the play behavior of the children in the Warsaw ghetto playground described by Jan Karski. In reading his description, we can almost see the hunger on the children's faces and sense the nervous energy emanating from the starving and traumatized children: "Children, every bone in their skeletons showing through their taut skins, played in heaps and swarms." Other descriptions of children also note an unnatural intensity in their behavior and responses.

The theory of arousal, however, falls short in providing a full explanation of the play urge either in normal circumstances or in the Holocaust. Just like the relatively recent ecological theory of play, it is able to account only for the content, format of play, and associated behavior. One of the strongest counterarguments is the fact that arousal-seeking play behavior was not an independent function. Arousal may have influenced the intensity and facilitation of play behavior, but it could not, by itself, propel one to engage in play—it could only govern its content and form. We must also acknowledge that the Holocaust provided such an aversive stress situation that in most instances no boredom could infiltrate the children's world. Exactly the opposite was true; the children were bombarded constantly with stressful stimuli. The actual interaction between child and environment must have been radically different in the Holocaust from what it was in artificially created and controlled situations. Finally, the arousal theory inevitably relegates the organism, in this case the children of the Holocaust, to a mere "reacting" entity. This notion is a complete negation of the idea of the organism as an "initiator" or a "primary mover." An organism, any organism, must respond continuously to environmental stimuli for survival. This is the adaptation syndrome. Humans, however, not only react to changes but also conscious-

17. Children's paintings from Theresienstadt show the imagination could transcend barbed wire. From an anonymous diary from Theresienstadt, 1942–43. Courtesy of Precious Legacy Project, Linda Altschuler, B'nai B'rith Klutznik Museum, Washington, D.C.

ly shape and adjust their environment. Play is an integral part of both their adaptation and the initiation syndrome.[26]

It is difficult to reach a conclusive explanation for why playing went on, even in the most inhuman conditions, in the sewers, in the childen's barracks of Auschwitz, and in the shadows of the crematoria. But, again, the theory of arousal offers only a vague and partial explanation for the content and behavior of play, leaving us to seek into the probability of a bioneurological activation. We might suppose, also, that a child, hungry and traumatized, made all attempts to reestablish a mental equilibrium through play. Thus games became especially precious when they were carried out in a symbolic or fantasy context. Many of the surviving pictures from Theresienstadt are scenes of frolic in playsettings. Yet we know that no real playground existed in the camp and that in order to engage in the kind of play shown the children's imagination had to transcend the barbed-wire fences. These pictures are arresting in the wish they express to stop time and carry the unfortunate children back to a happier present and place. They could not reflect the immediate present but only a fantasy world where anything could happen. The drawings show a fairy-tale land where flowers, swings, and

sandboxes are the backdrop for the smiles of children. These "play actions" would emerge with the cognitive intelligence of children for manipulating, rearranging, or transforming aspects of reality to their own mental world. It was mentioned earlier how a six-year-old girl who was hidden under a table in a hospital room could see only legs walking by. Her imagination transformed them into very small people. She "would manipulate all these people" like little dolls. Another girl, seven years old, was hidden in Auschwitz among corpses. She fantasized that she had a doll's head to play with. At first glance both girls' play urge seems almost wholly instinctual—the children were rearranging their immediate environments for the sake of coping with psychological stress. On the final account, however, it was the environment that provided both of them with the most powerful stimuli for a particular behavior. Thus the functional significance of fantasy-play did not rest in its offering an opportunity for the avoidance of coping with reality but in its ability to assist in "reality assimilation"—information processing in other words.[27]

Thus we might assume that this urge for coping, propelling the children to play even in the most perilous circumstances, was a part of an assimilation-accommodation complex. One of the most lucid arguments that supports this assumption has been advanced by Richard S. Lazarus, who reasoned that emotion can serve as a "coping response." He points out, independently from the issues of the Holocust or play, that the survival of individuals and groups requires effective adaptation to the dangers inherent in each environment. In order to survive, an individual has to be able to evaluate the presence or absence of danger and—if it exists—be able to formulate an effective response to it. Such an evaluation, recognition, or appraisal could determine later the coping impulse or accommodational response.[28]

It seems obvious that human play in the Holocaust possessed distinct functional properties. Whether the source of play was a need for stimulation, at least in dealing with the Holocaust, can be demonstrated only if the motive for arousal was presented by the encounters with the environment. This environment, however, required a constant need for adaptation and entailed processing information (assimilation) and consequent behavior modification (accommodation). Children do not simply copy or enact their universe even in normal circumstances, and that certainly did not happen in the Holocaust. The environmental conditions were so predominant in governing behavior that they inevitably overshadowed intrinsic activation, i.e., arousal, for play. Through play and games a certain buffered learning process was initiated which served to make children familiar with an otherwise alien universe and provided them with an ability to function in this universe.

Death, suffering, and pain were ubiquitous in the ghettos and camps. And we have seen that play in any culture cannot divorce itself from the reality in which it takes place. Consequently, many play forms and much of the play content and behavior assimilated within them the ecological factors that eminently governed them in the first place. Again, the children did not simply copy the atrocities surrounding them; rather, they imposed on reality their own constructions and interpretations. In fact, all surviving evidence indicates that the children had a clear grasp of reality and were aware of their fate. Play of the Holocaust, however, reflected this reality in a "bent" form, fitting the players' existing level of cognitive functioning. While it was not formulated for the specific question of play, Lazarus's theory provides us with important clues to understanding this mechanism. He discovered that in laboratory conditions stress was reduced by an "intellectualization" process—i.e., the process of appraising a traumatic situation. In this context the rationale that play could offer adaptive benefits by presenting one's experience in an acceptable form is quite plausible.

The theory Lazarus proposed cannot offer a complete explanation of the motivation of children for play in the Holocaust, especially because he did not propose it with the eventualities of the war in mind. One can, however, augment his rationale with the assumption that play and games also facilitated an "accommodation" process by which an organism could negotiate the novel demands of an absurd situation (as J. H. Flawell elaborated on Piaget's views about the function of play in general). Indeed, this "assimilation-accommodation" paradigm, as Flawell called it, is perhaps the most conceivable explanation for children's play in the Holocaust. "The organism adapts repeatedly," he wrote in 1963, "and each adaptation necessarily paves the way for its successor."[29]

A haunting question still remains to be answered: Do we enact in play what we are or do we become what we play? Although it will be discussed later, the play activities of Holocaust children, albeit not the most suitable for post-Holocaust life, prepared them for a future existence. In some ways, then, the survivors became what they played as children. We must also argue, as a survivor rationalized in retrospect, that playing was more than passing the time in a concentration camp. It helped her and many other children in Theresienstadt to clarify, rationalize, and accommodate reality, which was not amenable to other explanation. "What did the play mean? I'm not sure now, but I think I said it just now: it interchanged fantasy and reality so that we could at least try to survive."[30] Although the outcome of her Holocaust experience was unique—she survived—her comment represents other children's experiences. Play and games made a completely irrational reality more rational and, perhaps, more bearable.

Flawell's thoughts, although not formulated with the Holocaust in mind, also explain the content of Holocaust play and the play behavior associated with it. When the adult community could not provide a stable and rational environment, the children themselves had to create a world that was functional, rational, and sensible on their cognitive level. Upon their shoulders rested the burden of reestablishing a badly shattered equilibrium for which play was the most convenient medium. Indeed, play and games served the comprehension of an absurd situation (accommodation) in the Holocaust. Yet they could not fulfill the function indefinitely. First, it was impossible to elude the final fate. But, from our point of view, the physiological constraint of the absurd milieu that was the Holocaust decreed an insurmountable limitation to play. The fact that an utterly reduced fat content will alter the psychological responses of an individual to the environment was proved in the "human laboratories" of Auschwitz and other death camps. Recent animal experiments reinforced this conclusion by adding that all play activities also ceased with an *extended* food deprivation and suffering. When a child in the Holocaust reached a physiological stage of "Musselmann" (an Auschwitz term for the utterly exhausted skeletons), the inherent play urge, or the "assimilation-accommodation" paradigm, disappeared. With an utterly reduced body-fat content, the internal impulse to play ceased to function and the external stimuli that might have elicited play behavior were ignored.

That reinforces the recognition that play is not only a psychologically but also a physiologically regulated entity. The skeleton children, lying on the sidewalks of Warsaw and other ghettos, were beyond play. For them there was a point of no return when the body sank too low for the spirit to rise.

IN OUR WORLD view children possess an air of innocence. Clinging to innocent childhood, just like clinging to life or to a hope, is a reflection of humanity for us. The children of the Holocaust played, hoped, and succeeded in coping momentarily with ever-present death. But they saw everything that grown-ups saw. Fear came to them, as they told honestly in their poems and diaries.

I was once a little child,
Three years ago.
That child who longed for other words.
But now I am no more a child.
For I have learned to hate.
I am a grown up person now,
I have known fear.[31]

The constant accommodation was in itself no assurance that life would prevail. Perhaps they were more honest and perceptive than adults. The little toys, the see-saws, swings, and sandbox could not overcome human depravity, evil, misery, and death. But at least they helped children to accommodate themselves to atrocity. Nothing could express the anguish and pain of the Holocaust more painfully and literally than the following enactment of a tragedy beyond human scale—the capsulation of the Holocaust in the child's game. A teacher in the Lodz ghetto noticed a one-sided discussion between a little boy, whose whole family was already deported, and a five-year-old girl. "He was dawdling and talking loudly to himself, . . ." she wrote about the scene. "One hand was full of small stones. . . ."

> At first the boy dropped three small stones. They hit the ground with a slight sound, then two more, followed by another three. Next the little boy quickly closed his fist. In his lively eyes the shiny black pupils stopped their race for a moment. . . .
>
> "Nine brothers like these stones we were once, all close together. Then came the first deportation and three of the brothers didn't return, two were shot at the barbed wire fences and three died of hunger. Can you guess how many brother-stones are still left in my hand?"[32]

7
Epilogue

"I owe an explanation to my children"

AN OLD FRENCH proverb says that "a hundred thousand corpses is a statistic, but the death of a single human being remains an acute human pain." It has become almost a cliché that the Holocaust is a tragedy on a scale that no dramatist or artist has ever been able to express. Throughout the six years of the war, in the period of the greatest institutionalized slaughter known to humanity, more than a million Jewish children were exterminated. Behind the numbers of killed, incarcerated, and tortured there are gripping personal histories. Obviously, the numbers in themselves cannot provide an all-encompassing picture of the tragedy. It is doubtful that anything can. For every extant diary or testimony there are hundreds of thousands of victims who never had an opportunity to speak. Yet descriptions of children's play and interpretations of its meaning for different segments of the populace can provide at least a small glimpse into the many levels of human experiences in the Holocaust. The descriptions can also offer some explanations of the motivating factors governing human responses in stressful situations in general.

Yet an analytical and scholarly attitude in face of horrors and atrocities is a stance often beyond the ability of even a detached observer. One of the hardest tasks for a historian, chronicler, and storyteller is to transcend statistics and put faces and words to the incomprehensible numbers. Such an undertaking entails weaving cold facts and nightmarish oral histories into a human narrative that can lead the reluctant mind through the corners, recesses, and nooks of hell. Working at such project erodes any vestiges of objectivity, for the Holocaust confronts us with the most probing questions about our own humanity and values and about the capacity of humankind for inflicting and enduring suffering.

The references and narratives alluding to children's play during this period are not in themselves a broad enough base for making generalizations about all human experiences during the Holocaust. Indeed, the study of children's play provides only a narrow slice of the history of the Holocaust. Conversely, the Holocaust experience of play provides only a partial view of play in general, and even of play under adverse circumstances. There are many Vietnams, Cambodias, and El Salvadors that also must be investigated for a fuller comprehension of play under stress. The Holocaust, however, is able to provide us with enough information for a better understanding of human behavior under extreme deprivation and the role of play as a medium for negotiating the requirements for survival.

Children's play did not highlight or hide the shabbiness and decay of their surroundings. The environment of the children was not made invisible or more hospitable through the medium of play. Rather the scenery of bleakness became an integral part of their activity, a setting that was inevitable in the Holocaust. Although changing the backdrop was beyond their control, the children often succeeded, through the power of imagination and make-believe, in rising above reality. Indeed, their play was often an enactment of a tragedy with genuinely live actors—it presented a unique and highly condensed dramatic plot. In the larger Nazi scenario, the children suffered, anguished, and most of them died. But before they died some of them grasped a moment to comment on their lives—to improvise as real artists do. They wrote diaries and poems, they painted pictures, and they played games. They also knew that there would be no reprieve from the finale: "Don't cry Pista," a little Hungarian boy encouraged his friend en route to the gas chambers, "haven't you seen that our grandparents, our fathers, our mothers, and our sisters were killed? It is our turn now."[1]

PLAY IN THE Holocaust did not mean, indeed it could not mean, joy and happiness. The games children played were a microcosm of life, reduced from its complexities to a symbolic action. Although they played, the children suffered even in the most "human" camps, from many psychological disorders. Great weight losses, bitter weeping, bed-wetting, and mental regression can all be attributed to camp life. Yet the children reacted and rebounded, at least initially, faster and more creatively than the adults. The young people, and especially the children, possessed no strong roots in the past. They were less attached to conventional values and norms—they floated, as a survivor poetically phrased it, like a "leaf in the wind." It is beyond doubt that their play and games had a significant role in their accommodation to the Holocaust existence.

18. Two Hungarian boys stand bewildered on the Auschwitz platform, 1944. Courtesy of the Simon Wiesenthal Center, Los Angeles, Calif.

Some questions remain to be answered. Among the most obvious is, What happened to the precious few who survived? How did those children adjust to their new conditions and realities in a post-Holocaust era? Did Holocaust play activities have any role in their ability to regain their mental and emotional equilibrium? Answers to these questions are just now beginning to surface as a consequence of related psychological research. Basically, however, very little has been written on children's experiences in the Holocaust or the repercussions of those experiences for the survivors' further developments.

For the children just emerging from the shadows of the Holocaust, the future was full of physical uncertainties as well as moral and mental ambiguities. The short- and long-range effects of years of deprivation, fear, and suffering stamped an indelible mark upon the psyche of the survivors.[2] Of course the immediate impact was generally the most dramatic. After leaving a bunker with his mother, a nine-year-old boy looked around the world with puzzlement: "I couldn't walk, and the sunlight burned my eyes. . . . The joy of liberation was so great that I didn't have the strength to really feel the happiness that from this time on I would be able to live like other children."

The comment of a little girl, who had just come out of the sewers of Lvov with her younger brother, rings heartbreakingly similar:

> Neither I nor my brother looked like normal children. . . . I could not have enough of the bright sunshine, of the flowers and of everything out in the open. But my brother Pavel cried, he was fearful and dragged us back to the sewer because he was not used to the normal world. I never knew till now such joy and good fortune as to fill myself with the bright, clear world around me, where the sun also shines for me and the flowers spread their scent also for me.

With some caution one might deduce from survivors' accounts that with the elation of liberation, a mixture of seething rage and frustration also burned within the newly freed children. Following years of incarceration and hiding it was perhaps natural. Another little girl's instinct led her to run wildly down the slopes, but having not been outdoors for over a year she found she could not climb back up the hill. As she pondered the situation several decades later she still remembered the pain and "the feeling of frustration and anger that here I finally could run and could do and [yet] hurt so much."[3]

The children who spent time in hiding could never forget their experiences. Yet if it is possible to rate degrees of misery and mental pain, these youngsters suffered less than their counterparts who had to endure the concentration and death camps of Nazi Europe. For them there had been no escape. After liberation the children preoccupied themselves with death—fear, nightmares, and crying through the night became permanent experiences. More impressive than all the psychological research about human trauma was the case of a young boy who after liberation knew only one game—burying corpses. These children were unable to play standard games or to relate to playmates. A young girl who arrived in Auschwitz as a toddler never mastered violent fits of rage and years after her liberation they would still appear: "Suddenly in the middle of the best game, she jumped at other children, beat them, yelled and then again she was quiet and shy."[4]

There were also long-term effects that followed the young prisoners, bursting forth well after the liberation during psychiatric treatments. A young woman in her late twenties resigned herself to the unavoidable fact that camp memories would never fade. "In the midst of some game" she suddenly became covered with cold sweat. She had to face the realization that "there is no cure for that" (i.e., the Holocaust). The consequences of an existence in the ghettos, camps, and hiding places had latent effects upon the children's psyche as well. In talking to me, a survivor from Belgium realized suddenly, and noted it with a hazy mist in her eyes, that she lost her childhood and the loss made her unprepared for motherhood and normal relations with her own children. It came to her that she had not learned or mastered, among the necessary skills of parenting, the art of play. It is plausible that a genetically regulated motivational instinct exists that thrusts parents into play activities with their children. Through play the parental organism attempts to convey a genetic knowledge that provides the future generation with the ability for information processing and problem solving. The medium of play enables the parents to pass onto the young the capacity to establish or restore physio-psychological equilibrium in a constantly changing world. The conditions for these processes were obviously absent during the Holocaust. Although not scientifically expressed, another survivor's comments about her experiences during the Holocaust and their repercussions in later life conveyed similar message:

> I don't even feel I know how to play and I found that it's a very big lack with my own children and I think my mother had a wonderful experience because, and I envy her, because she can play all these games with my kids and I somehow was able to do educational stuff with them, read to them, but I couldn't play, because I don't think I ever played, and I really believe play is a learned thing. I mean you have to play to know how to play.[5]

Psychologists might justifiably argue that play activities of concentration camps provided the children with neither the skills nor the values for a post-Holocaust existence. Laboratory experiments with primates show that social isolation and associated play deprivation invariably result in maladapted individuals with some form of emotional disorder. Playing involves learned behavior—at least as far as content and subject are concerned. The tragedy of the children who spent years behind barbed wire is that they could not play the usual "childish" games. When a concerned adult explained in the Berga-Elster concentration camp the essence of "Cowboys and Indians" to ten-year-olds, the children were not impressed by the game, which they termed "silly" or "disgusting." Their game was "watching the SS-man."

> They watched them beat people, kick people, torture people, kill people. Indeed, they needed no aggressive play. Reality mirrored their fantasy life. What other children in normal society act out through play, these children *witnessed in reality*.[6]

Disregarding for a moment the major traumas and shocks these children survived, there is something eerie about this kind of account. It reaffirms the idea that the play that was possible under the circumstances of the Holocaust left a whole generation—decimated as it was—unprepared for postwar roles as parents. The testimonies of the survivors are a common enough phenomenon, as psychologists have discovered, among people in child survivor groups. Many victims indicated what my interviewee realized, that they could not play with their own children for they never learned how to play.

We can see that play should be considered neither an innocent and trivial matter nor an accidental occurrence. In the Holocaust, it became an instinctual form for understanding the absurd and for accommodating the irrational. Play, with its unique conflict-resolving qualities, also provided the children with a mental mechanism that facilitated their ability to cope with the psychological and physical environment. That it could not provide the most precious of all promises, the promise of survival, is almost inconsequential. Nothing could provide this promise. The children suffered, cried, laid down their broken bodies and died: sometimes they played. They played for the few moments they were given with the vehemence and desperation that only the doomed can have. Their images loom starkly in front of our eyes. Indeed, images help us understand and memories help us preserve the world revolving around us. The figures of children playing with the backdrop of ruined homes and glowing skies over the camps should be one of these images. They are metaphors that can assist us in comprehending the depth of human evil. The story of their play in the Holocaust is only one of the many stories—there are others that perhaps will never be told—and even this picture is somewhat fragmented and incomplete, but at least it reflects a part of Holocaust reality. It, however, also carries the message that children's play is a reflection of humanity and that ultimately, humanity and inhumanity are reflected in children.

The pictures of these suffering and tormented children transcend time, space, race, and creed. They remind us that children are the most defenseless victims of all wars—moving out of this world silently—just like the last walk of the little Polish children in Auschwitz. Olga Lengyel, an inmate, could not forget these little images as they "staggered toward death," resigned, exhausted, terrified, and sprinkled with white flakes: "They were silent under the blows, silent like so many little snowmen."[7]

Appendix A
List of Ghettos and Nazi Camps Mentioned in This Book

Ghettos and various Nazi camps constituted a web of highly diversified and varied institutions. Many of their differences can be attributed to local conditions, individual commandants, and, of course, the Nazi designs for these places. Their names are spelled in the bibliography alternately in Yiddish, German, and the native language, depending on the source.

Ghettos

Bialystok—Poland
Cracow—Poland
Kaunas (Kovno in Hebrew)—Lithuania
Lodz (Litzmanstadt in German)—Poland
Lublin—Poland
Marysin—a semi-rural suburb of Lodz
Riga—Latvia
Siaulaui (Shavli in Hebrew)—Lithuania
Sosnowitz—Poland
Vilna—Lithuania
Warsaw—Poland

Nazi Camps

Transit Camps

Drancy—camp for foreign-born and French Jews, France
Gur—camp for foreign-born Jews, France

Transit Camps (cont.)

Rivesaltes—camp for foreign-born and French Jews, France
Vugh—camp for Dutch Jews, Holland
Westerbork—camp for Dutch Jews, Holland

Labor Camps

Plaszow—located near Cracow, Poland

Concentration Camps

Berga-Elster—subcamp attached to Buchenwald, Germany
Bergen Belsen—close to Hannover, Germany
Buchenwald—close to Weimar, Germany
Neuengamme—close to Hamburg, Germany
Ravensbrueck—a women's camp, Germany
Theresienstadt (Terezin in Czech)—a fortress town, Bohemia

Extermination Camps

Chelmno—camp located in the center of Poland; place where the Lodz ghetto inhabitants were killed
Treblinka—camp where large percentage of the Jews of Warsaw perished, Poland

Labor/Extermination Camps

Auschwitz/Birkenau—camp near Cracow, Poland
Majdanek—camp near Lublin, Poland

Appendix B
List of Persons

Auerbach, Rachel—Warsaw ghetto diarist
Auserwald, Heinz—Nazi kommissar of the Warsaw ghetto
Berg, Mary—Young diarist in the Warsaw ghetto who succeeded in reaching America during the war
Borowski, Tadeusz—Polish inmate of Auschwitz, author
Czerniakow, Adam—Head of the Warsaw Judenrat; he committed suicide at the commencement of the mass deportation of the Warsaw Jewry
David, Janina—Child survivor of the Holocaust; she wrote a moving book of her experiences in the Warsaw ghetto
Eichmann, Adolf—German officer entrusted with the collection and deportation of European Jewry to death camps; he was executed in Israel in 1962
Frank, Anne—Young diarist from Amsterdam who died in Bergen Belsen; she became famous for her touching diary
Frank, Hans—Governor-general of part of Nazi-occupied Poland; he was convicted of war crimes and executed in Nuremberg
Gemmeker, Albert—Commandant of Westerbork; he was sentenced to ten years imprisonment after the war
Gens, Jacob—Head of the Vilna Judenrat
Goebbels, Josef—Propaganda minister of the Third Reich; he committed suicide at the end of the war
Goeth, Amon—Commandant of Plaszow; he was executed after the war
Goldstein, Bernard—Bundist leader in Warsaw; he survived the war in hiding
Hart, Kitty—Auschwitz prisoner, author
Hirsch, Freddy—Educator and youth leader in Theresienstadt and later in the Family Camp of Auschwitz; he died in 1943

Hoess, Rudolf—Commandant of Auschwitz; he was executed for his crimes
Jakubowicz, Mira—Educator and playground supervisor in the Warsaw ghetto
Kalmanowitch, Zelig—Educator and diarist from Vilna
Kaplan, Chaim—Educator and diarist in the Warsaw ghetto; he died in Treblinka
Karski, Jan—A courier of the Polish underground who provided a thorough account of the horrors in a 1944 book
Kautsky, Benedict—Statesman and later an Auschwitz prisoner
Korczak, Janusz—Well-known physician and educator in Warsaw; he died in Treblinka with the children of his orphanage
Krause, Wilhelm Karl—Commandant of the Riga ghetto
Kulka, Erik—Auschwitz survivor, author
Levin, Abraham—Educator and diarist in Warsaw; he died in Treblinka
Levy-Haas, Hanna—Diarist, a Yugoslav inmate in Bergen-Belsen
Mechanicus, Philip—Dutch journalist and diarist in Westerbork; he died in Auschwitz
Muszkat, Joseph—Jewish police officer in Vilna; he organized a children's brigade from orphans in the ghetto
Ohlendorf, Otto—Commandant of one of the Einsatzkommandos (mobile killing units)
Remba, Nachum—Warsaw Judenrat official; he died in Treblinka
Ringelblum, Emmanuel—Historian; he established a secret archive in the Warsaw ghetto; he died in hiding
Rosenfeld, Oskar—Diarist in Lodz ghetto
Rudashevski, Yitshok—Young diarist from the Vilna ghetto; he died in a labor camp
Rumkowski, Chaim—The "Eldest of the Jews"; (chairman) of the Lodz Judenrat; he was deported and killed in Auschwitz
Schalkova, Malvina—Theresienstadt painter; she died in Auschwitz
Silkes, Genia—Teacher in the Warsaw ghetto
Silten, Gabriele—Survivor of the Westerbork and Theresienstadt camps
Székely, Éva—Hungarian Olympic swimming champion
Troller, Norbert—Artist incarcerated in Theresienstadt
Vrba, Rudolf—Auschwitz prisoner who succeeded in escaping the camp and alerting the world to the mass exterminations
Zabludowicz, Noah—Holocaust survivor and witness at the Eichman trial

Notes

1 : Prologue

1. Cited in Rudolf Vrba and Alan Bestic, *I Cannot Forgive* (New York: Grove Press, 1964), p. 54.

2. G. M. Gilbert, *Nuremberg Diary* (New York: Signet Books, 1961), p. 354.

3. The highest estimate of the number of children exterminated was given as 1,200,000 in Mark Dworzecki, *Europa Lelo Yeladim* (Jerusalem: Yad Vashem, 1958), p. 56; Kiryl Shoshnowski, *The Tragedy of Children under Nazi Rule* (Poznan: Zachonia, 1962), pp. 70–75. In scholarly literature the terms *ghetto* and *camp* are used interchangeably in the case of Theresienstadt.

4. In his study of the Holocaust, Lawrence L. Langer addresses many of the inherent historiographical problems in investigating the Holocaust; see *Versions of Survival: The Holocaust and the Human Spirit* (Albany: State University of New York Press, 1982), pp. 4–8; see also the insightful and critical work of Lucy S. Dawidowicz, *The Holocaust and the Historians* (Cambridge: Harvard University Press, 1981).

5. Langer, *Versions of Survival*, p. 129.

6. Johan Huizinga, *Homo Ludens* (New York: Routledge and Kegan Paul, 1949), p. 13.

7. This quote has been selected from Stanislaw Rozycki's *Warsaw Ghetto Diary*, which seems to have been written in the fall of 1941. The present translation is based on excerpts published in *Faschismus—Getto—Massenmord: Dokumentation ueber Ausrottung und Widerstand der Juden in Polen waehrend des 2. Weltkrieges*, ed. Zydowski Instytut Historyczny, Warsaw (Frankfurt/Main, 1962), pp. 152–56. Quoted in Ulrich Keller, ed. *The Warsaw Ghetto in Photographs* (New York: Dover, 1984), p. 130.

8. Mihaly Csikszentmihalyi, "Some Paradoxes in the Definition of Play," in *Play as Context*, ed. Alyce Taylor Cheska (West Point, N.Y.: Leisure Press, 1981), pp. 14–25.

9. Quoted in Hermann Langbeim, *Menschen in Auschwitz* (Wien: Europaverlag, 1972), p. 37; also in Langer, *Versions of Survival*, p. 6.
10. Thomas Keneally, *Schindler's List* (New York: Penguin Books, 1983), p. 269; Gertrude Schneider, *Journey into Terror: Story of the Riga Ghetto* (New York: Ark House, 1979), pp. 118–19; see also Eric H. Boehm, *We Survived: The Stories of the Hidden and the Hunted of Nazi Germany* (Santa Barbara, Calif.: Clio Press, 1966), p. 270.
11. Huizinga, *Homo Ludens*, p. 45.
12. See Robert Fagen, "Modeling How and Why Play Works," in *Play: Its Role in Development and Evolution*, ed. Jerome S. Burner et al. (New York: Basic Books, 1976), pp. 96–115; P. V. Gump and Brian Sutton-Smith, "Activity-Setting and Social Interaction," *American Journal of Orthopsychiatry* 25 (1955):755–60; S. B. Sells, "An Interactionist Looks at the Environment," *American Psychologist* (1963):696–702; Joseph Levy, *Play Behavior* (New York: John Wiley and Sons, 1978), pp. 124–35.
13. Paul Trepman, *Among Men and Beasts*, trans. Shoshana Perla and Gertrude Hirschler (New York: A. S. Barnes, 1978), p. 194. Trepman was a close acquaintance of Mira Jakubowicz.

2 : The Child in the Holocaust

1. Gideon Hausner, *Justice in Jerusalem* (New York: Harper and Row, 1966), p. 163; see also L. Poliakov, "The Mind of the Mass Murderer," *Commentary* 12 (November 1951):451–59.
2. Otto Ohlendorf's testimony was made in front of the military tribunal of the Allied governments. Quoted by Nora Levin, *The Holocaust* (New York: Thomas Y. Crowell, 1968), pp. 242–43.
3. Three affidavits of Hermann Friedrich Grbe, November 10 and 13, 1945, including eyewitness accounts of the slaughter of Jews in Dubno and Rovno, Ukraine. See Levin, *Holocaust*, p. 265; quoted by Endre Sós, *Europai Fasizmus és Antiszemitizmus* (Budapest: Magyar Téka, n.d.), pp. 121–22.
4. It is instructive to note that earlier warnings for the Jews of the ghetto, issued by the Gestapo in July, clearly stated the death penalty for pregnant women as well as their families. Similar policies were enforced in other ghettos and labor camps in Poland, Lithuania, and Latvia. Eliezer Yerushalmi, *Pinkas Shavli* (Jerusalem: Yad Vashem, 1958), pp. 96–97.
5. Quoted by Shoshnowski, *Tragedy of Children*, p. 71; Stanislawa Leszczunska, "Report of a Midwife from Auschwitz," and Janina Kosciuszkowa, "Children in the Auschwitz Concentration Camp," in *Auschwitz, An Anthology on Inhuman Medicine* (Warsaw: International Auschwitz Committee, 1971), 2:181–227; Thomas Geve, *Youth in Chains* (Jerusalem: Rubin Mass, 1981), p. 203. The existence of children's blocks in Auschwitz/Birkenau, Buchenwald, and other camps, especially after 1943, is now beyond doubt. See *Newsletter of the Jerome Riker International Study of Organized Persecution of Children* (Spring and Fall 1987).
6. Serge Klarsfeld, ed., *Les enfants d'Izieu une tragédie juive* (The Beate Klarsfeld Foundation, 1983); Keneally, *Schindler's List*, pp. 259–63; see also Yitshok Rudashevski, *The Diary of the Vilna Ghetto*, trans. Percy Matenko (Tel Aviv: Shamgar Press, 1973);

and Yerushalmi, *Pinkas Shavli,* p. 302. By June 1942, the knowledge of children's extermination became widespread, as Emmanuel Ringelblum's notes from the Warsaw ghetto demonstrate (*Notes from the Warsaw Ghetto,* ed. Jacob Sloan [New York: Schocken Books, 1974], pp. 292–93).

7. Ben Edelbaum, *Growing Up in the Holocaust* (Kansas City: Ben Edelman, 1980), pp. 91–92.

8. Abraham Levin, *Me-Pinkaso shel ha-More me-Yehudiyah* (Tel Aviv: Hakibbutz Hameuchad, 1969), p. 34.

9. From Rozycki's diary, quoted in Keller, *Warsaw Ghetto in Photographs,* p. 129. There are differing views as to the actual number of fatalities related to hunger. See Lucy L. Dawidowicz, *The War against the Jews, 1933–1945* (New York: Holt, Rinehart and Winston, 1975), p. 214, and Isaiah Trunk, "Epidemics and Mortality in the Warsaw Ghetto, 1939–1942," *YIVO Annual of Jewish Social Sciences* 8 (1953):82–122.

10. Mary Berg, *Warsaw Ghetto Diary,* ed. S. L. Shneiderman (New York: L. B. Fischer, 1945), p. 66.

11. Chaim A. Kaplan, *The Warsaw Diary of Chaim Kaplan,* trans. Abraham I. Katch (New York: Collier Books, 1973), p. 290; quoted by Dawidowicz, *War against the Jews,* p. 215.

12. Halina Szwambaum, "Four Letters from the Warsaw Ghetto," *Commentary* 31 (June 1961):491. From Rozycki's *Warsaw Ghetto Diary,* quoted in Keller, *Warsaw Ghetto in Photographs,* p. 130.

13. Similar impressions were recorded by many observers of the ghetto universe. Tosha Bialer, "Behind the Wall," *Collier's,* February 20, 1943, p. 18. For the Lodz ghetto, see Lucjan Dobroszycki, ed., *The Chronicle of the Lodz Ghetto, 1941–1944* (New Haven: Yale University Press, 1984), pp. 344, 470–71.

14. Isaiah Trunk, *Lodzher Geto* (New York: YIVO Institute, 1962), p. 343; Kaplan, *Warsaw Diary,* p. 322; see also Ringelblum, *Notes from the Warsaw Ghetto,* p. 125.

15. David Rubinowicz, *The Diary of David Rubinowicz,* trans. Derek Bowman (Edmonds, Wash.: Creative Options, 1982), p. 61; Rudashevski, *Diary of the Vilna Ghetto,* p. 32.

16. Interview with Daisy Miller, April 10, 1986.

17. Marie Syrkin, *Blessed Is the Match* (New York: Alfred A. Knopf, 1947), p. 181; Rudashevski, *Diary of the Vilna Ghetto,* p. 32.

18. Dawidowicz, *War against the Jews,* p. 212.

19. Trunk, *Lodzher Geto,* p. 340; Bernard Goldstein, *The Stars Bear Witness* (New York: Viking Press, 1949), p. 62. Goldstein was a widely respected leader of the Socialist Labor Union, the Bund, in Poland.

20. Berg, *Warsaw Ghetto Diary,* p. 87.

21. For an exhaustive and objective treatment of the functions and activities of Jewish councils in Eastern Europe, see Isaiah Trunk, *Judenrat: The Jewish Councils in Eastern Europe under the Nazi Occupation* (New York: Macmillan, 1972). The fact that Rumkowski was the director of an orphanage before the war may explain the attention and affection he gave to orphans. See Solomon F. Bloom, "Dictator of the Lodz Ghetto," *Commentary* 7 (February 1949):111–22, and Philip Friedman, "Two 'Saviors' Who Failed," *Commentary* 26 (May 1958):479–91.

22. Although no source besides Kaplan's *Warsaw Diary* (p. 184) mentions a "Children's Month" in August 1940, it seems likely that a drive did take place on a small scale. Initially, Ringelblum was much more critical of the campaign than any other source, exhibiting a clear political bias against the Judenrat and what it stood for. See *Notes from the Warsaw Ghetto*, p. 234.
23. One of the best sources on welfare efforts in Eastern European ghettos is Trunk, *Judenrat*, chap. 6.
24. Alexander Donat, *The Holocaust Kingdom: A Memoir* (New York: Holocaust Library, 1978), p. 12. The original source, it seems, was Emmanuel Ringelblum.
25. Rudashevski, *Diary of the Vilna Ghetto*, p. 92.

3 : Play and the Community

1. From Rozycki, *Warsaw Ghetto Diary*, quoted by Keller, *Warsaw Ghetto in Photographs*, pp. 130–31.
2. Gerhard Schoenberner, *The Yellow Star: The Persecution of the Jews in Europe. 1933–1945*, trans. Susan Sweet (New York: Bantam Books, 1979), p. 51.
3. From Rozycki, *Warsaw Ghetto Diary*, quoted by Keller, *Warsaw Ghetto in Photographs*, p. 130; H. Volikova, *I Never Saw Another Butterfly: Children's Drawings and Poems from Terezin Concentration Camp, 1942–1944* (New York: McGraw-Hill, 1964); the sentimental song was quoted by Dawidowicz, *War against the Jews*, p. 208.
4. Éva Székely, *Sirni Csak a Gyöztesnek Szabad* (Budapest: Magvetö, 1982), pp. 28–29; Gerda Klein-Weissman, *All But My Life* (New York: Hill and Wang, 1957), pp. 43, 49; Yitzhak Arad, *Ghetto in Flames* (New York: Holocaust Library, 1982), p. 95; Jacob Presser, *The Destruction of the Dutch Jews*, trans. Arnold Pomerans (New York: E. P. Dutton, 1969), pp. 83–85; Kaplan, *Warsaw Diary*, pp. 173, 220.
5. Presser, *Destruction of the Dutch Jews*, p. 89; Anny Latour, *The Jewish Resistance in France*, trans. Irene R. Ilton (New York: Holocaust Library, 1981), pp. 38–39.
6. Székely, *Sirni Csak a Gyöztesnek Szabad*, pp. 28–29.
7. Adam Czerniakow, *The Warsaw Diary of Adam Czerniakow*, ed. Raul Hilberg, Stanislaw Staron, and Josef Kermisz (New York: Stein and Day, 1979), p. 182.
8. Kaplan, who evinced no sympathy for Czerniakow, also lamented the loss of the Krasinski park. See *Warsaw Diary*, p. 352.
9. Dobroszycki, *Chronicle of the Lodz Ghetto*, p. 352.
10. Gerald Green, *The Artists of Terezin* (New York: Hawthorn Books, 1969), p. 139.
11. Janina David, *A Square of Sky* (New York: W. W. Norton, 1964), pp. 107–8.
12. Rachel Auerbach, *Be'hutzot Warsaw* (Tel Aviv: Am Oved, 1946), p. 43.
13. Kaplan, *Warsaw Diary*, p. 220; Nachman Blumenthal, *Darko Shel Yudnrat* (Jerusalem: Yad Vashem, 1962), pp. 166, 438, 452.
14. Emilia Gutman File, Genia Silkes Collection, YIVO Archives, New York; Berg, *Warsaw Ghetto Diary*, p. 148. While Berg's note was written in the spring of 1942, this custom became widespread at least a year earlier; Kaplan, *Warsaw Diary*, p. 353.
15. Ringelblum, *Notes from the Warsaw Ghetto*, p. 188; David, *Square of Sky*, p. 151.
16. For "Children's Corners," see Sarah Neshamit, *Ma'avako shel ha-Geto* (Lochamei Hagetaot: Hakibbutz Hameuchad, 1972), pp. 35, 77; Kaplan, *Warsaw Diary*, p. 294; Berg, *Warsaw Ghetto Diary*, p. 148.

17. Goldstein, *Stars Bear Witness,* p. 83.
18. Sylvia Rothchild, ed., *Voices from the Holocaust* (New York: New American Library, 1981), pp. 254–55; Goldstein, *Stars Bear Witness,* p. 84.
19. Trunk, *Lodzher Geto,* p. 62; Adolf Berman, "Goral Hayeladim Be-geto Warsaw," in *Sho'at Yehude Europah,* ed. Israel Gutman and Livia Rothkirchen (Jerusalem: Yad Vashem, 1973), pp. 294–308. This document was deposited in the Ringelblum Archives which aimed to salvage all documentary and literary evidence during the Holocaust about the destruction of Polish Jewry. Quoted in Aryeh Bauminger et al., *Hayeled ve-Hano'ar be-Shoah ve-be-Gevurah* (Jerusalem: Kiryat Sefer, 1965), pp. 55–56. See also Jonas Turkow, *Haya Hayta Warsaw Yehudit* (Tel Aviv: Tarbut Vehinuch, 1969), pp. 95–96.
20. L. Brenner, *Widershtand un umkum fun Czenstokhover Geto* (Warsaw, 1951), pp. 51–53; Kalmanowitch, "Diary of the Nazi Ghetto in Vilna," p. 25; Korczak is quoted in Lucy S. Dawidowicz, ed., *A Holocaust Reader* (New York: Behrman House, 1976), p. 194.
21. Auserwald in a memo to Dr. von Madeaazza, deputy of the Plenipotentiary of the Generalgouverneur, November 24, 1941, Yad Vashem Archives, Jerusalem, Microfilm Collection, JM 1112.
22. Berg, *Warsaw Ghetto Diary,* p. 147.
23. Trunk, *Lodzher Geto,* p. 343 (Document no. 115); Kaplan, *Warsaw Diary,* p. 353.
24. Kaplan, *Warsaw Diary,* p. 354.
25. Sara Zyskind, *Stolen Years* (Minneapolis: Lerner, 1981), pp. 89–90; Dobroszycki, *Chronicle of the Lodz Ghetto,* pp. 49–50; Bendet Hershkovitch, "The Ghetto in Litzmannstadt (Lodz)," *YIVO Annual of Jewish Social Sciences* 4(1950):94, in the Lodz Collection, YIVO Archives, New York.
26. Czerniakow, *Warsaw Diary,* p. 366.
27. This supervisor was Mira Jakubowicz at the playground at 21 Grzybowska Street. Quoted in Trepman, *Among Men and Beasts,* pp. 193–95.
28. Philip Mechanicus, *Year of Fear: A Jewish Prisoner Waits for Auschwitz,* trans. Irene S. Gibbons (New York: Hawthorn, 1968), pp. 145, 150.
29. Josef Katz, *One Who Came Back: The Diary of a Jewish Survivor,* trans. Hilda Reach (New York: Herzl Press, 1973), p. 59; Schneider, *Journey into Terror,* p. 37.
30. Eli Bachner, "Be-Theresienstadt, be-Mahane ha-Mishpachti be-Auschwitz, bein ha-Sonderkommando, be-Buchenwald," *Yalkut Moreshet* 22 (November 1976):84; H. G. Adler, *Theresienstadt, 1941–1945* (Tuebingen: J.C.B. Mohr, 1955), pp. 553, 241; Jacob Jacobson, *Terezin: The Daily Life, 1943–1945* (London: Jewish Central Information Office, 1946), p. 14.
31. See Filip Mueller, *Eyewitness in Auschwitz: Three Years in the Gas Chambers* (New York: Stein and Day, 1979); Mary S. Constanza, *The Living Witness: Art in the Concentration Camps and Ghettos* (New York: Free Press, 1981), p. 40; Bachner, "Be-Theresienstadt. . . . ," pp. 78–79, 85; Hanna Hofmann-Fischel Report, p. 9, Yad Vashem Archives, Jerusalem; Vrba and Bestic, *I Cannot Forgive,* pp. 181–82.
32. Hanna Hofmann-Fischel Report, Yad Vashem Archives, Jerusalem; Guenther Schwarberg, *The Murders at Bullenhuser Dam,* trans. Erna Baber Rosenfeld and Alvin H. Rosenfeld (Bloomington: Indiana University Press, 1984), pp. 9–17.
33. Through the heroic efforts of the Oeuvre du Secours aux Enfants (Relief Organi-

zation for Children), hundreds of children were rescued from these camps. See Latour, *Jewish Resistance in France;* Konzentrationslager Camp des Mills File, Leo Baeck Institute, New York.

34. Goldstein, *Stars Bear Witness,* p. 85.

35. Turkow, *Haya Hayta Warsaw Yehudit,* p. 96; Mark Dworzecki, *Yerushaleyim D'Lita be-Meri va-Shoah* (Tel Aviv: Mifleget Poalei Eretz-Yisrael, 1951), p. 219.

36. Vrba and Bestic, *I Cannot Forgive,* p. 182.

37. The July 19th entry was two days before the commencement of mass deportations. Czerniakow, *Warsaw Diary,* pp. 364, 382.

38. Jacob Boas, *Boulevard des Misères: The Story of Transit Camp Westerbork* (Hamden, Conn.: Archon Books, 1985), pp. 72–73.

39. Blumenthal, *Darko shel Yudnrat,* pp. 166, 452; Trunk, *Judenrat,* p. 210; Dworzecki, *Yerushalayim d'Lita,* p. 228.

40. Hershkovitch, "Ghetto in Litzmannstadt," p. 94; Lodz Collection, YIVO Archives, New York.

41. Yerushalmi, *Pinkas Shavli,* pp. 239, 242, 279.

42. See also chapter 2 above for a description of the Gesundheitsaktion in the Plaszow camp. Bertha Ferderber-Salz, *And the Sun Kept Shining* (New York: Holocaust Library, 1980), pp. 96–97; quoted in Dawidowicz, *War against the Jews,* p. 307; David Wolf File, Genia Silkes Collection, YIVO Archives, New York.

43. For a description of Janusz Korczak's last walk, see Yitzhak Zuckerman and Moshe Basok, eds., *Sefer Milhamot Hagetaot* (Tel Aviv: Hakibbutz Hameuchad, 1954), pp. 98–100.

44. Fredka Mazia, *Re'im Ba-sa'ar* (Jerusalem: Yad Vashem, 1964), pp. 125–28 (unfortunately, her fears were well founded. The nursery was raided); Ferderber-Salz, *And the Sun Kept Shining,* p. 68.

45. Czerniakow, *Warsaw Diary,* pp. 373–74.

46. Kaplan, *Warsaw Diary,* p. 244. (Similar sentiments were expressed by Gertrud Schneider in the Riga ghetto; see *Journey into Terror,* pp. 118–19); Mechanicus, *Year of Fear,* pp. 129, 159.

47. Levy-Haas, *Inside Belsen,* p. 17.

48. Saul Ash, "The Dignity of the Destroyed: Towards a Definition of the Period of the Holocaust," *Judaism* 2 (1962): 166.

49. Levy-Haas, *Inside Belsen,* p. 15; Kalmanowitch, "A Diary of the Nazi Ghetto of Vilna," pp. 25–26; Czerniakow, *Warsaw Diary,* pp. 376–77.

4 : Play and the Children

1. *Children's Drawings from the Concentration Camp of Terezin* (Prague: State Jewish Museum, n.d.), p. 14.

2. Dworzecki, *Yerushalayim D'Lita,* p. 232.

3. Christine Shigar File, Genia Silkes Collection, YIVO Archives, New York; Genia Silkes comments were recorded by Saul S. Friedman, *Amcha: An Oral Testament of the Holocaust* (Washington, D.C.: University Press of America), p. 137.

4. Levy-Haas, *Inside Belsen,* p. 249.

5. Quoted in Azriel Eisenberg, ed. *Witness to the Holocaust* (New York: Pilgrim Press,

1981), pp. 340–41; Bachner, "Be-Theresienstadt. . . . ," pp. 77–79; Alfred Kantor, *The Book of Alfred Kantor* (New York: McGraw-Hill, 1971), notes for plate 21.

6. Syrkin, *Blessed Is the Match*, p. 182.

7. Christina Shigar File, Genia Silkes Collection, YIVO Archives, New York. The original source is located in the Archive Central Jewish Historical Commission (no. 2352), Warsaw. Quoted also by Eisenberg, *Witness to the Holocaust*, p. 341.

8. David Wolf File, Genia Silkes Collection, YIVO Archives, New York.

9. Nelly Toll, *Without Surrender: Art of the Holocaust* (Philadelphia: Running Press, 1978), p. 94.

10. Ephraim Shtenkler, "What Happened to Me in My Childhood," *Commentary* 9 (May 1952):443.

11. Kaplan, *Warsaw Diary*, pp. 156, 244; Ringelblum, *Notes from the Warsaw Ghetto*, p. 168.

12. Geve, *Youth in Chains*, p. 97.

13. Kitty Hart, *I Am Alive* (Bakerville, Gt. Britain: Congi Books, 1961), pp. 92–93.

14. Ota Kraus and Erik Kulka, *Bet Haroshet le-Mavet: Auschwitz* (Jerusalem: Yad Vashem, 1960/61), p. 105.

15. Rudolf Hoess, *Commandant of Auschwitz*, trans. Constantin Fitz-Gibbon (Cleveland: World, 1959), pp. 170–71.

16. *Terezin* (Prague: Council of Jewish Communities in the Czech Lands, 1965), p. 92.

17. Interview with Daisy Miller, April 10, 1986.

18. Oskar Rosenfeld was a permanent contributor to the official records of the Lodz ghetto. Many of his brief entries dealt with everyday occurrences in the ghetto. Quoted in Dobroszycki, *Chronicle of the Lodz Ghetto*, pp. 360–61.

19. Ibid., pp. 373–74.

20. The story of the child from Kielce is from Helen Rosenzweig's recollections; Friedman, *Amcha*, p. 150; Sara Moskovitz, *Love Despite Hate* (New York: Schocken Books, 1983), p. 139.

21. Quoted in Ina R. Friedman, ed. *Escape or Die: True Stories of Young People Who Survived the Holocaust* (Reading, Mass.: Addison-Wesley, 1982), p. 61; interview with Gabriele Silten, February 17, 1986.

22. Interview with Gabriele Silten, February 17, 1986; interview with Daisy Miller, April 10, 1986. Miller's family was hidden for a year by Italian partisans in the hills of Tuscany.

23. Mechanicus, *Year of Fear*, p. 150; Jacobson, *Terezin*, p. 12; David, *Square of Sky*, p. 167.

24. Donat, *Holocaust Kingdom*, p. 23; interview with Gabriele Silten.

25. Quoted in Irving Halperin, *Messengers from the Death* (Philadelphia: Westminster Press, 1970), p. 134.

26. Auerbach, *Be'hutzot Warsaw*, p. 43; David Wolf File, Genia Silkes Collection, YIVO Archives, New York.

27. Sheva Glas-Wiener, *Children of the Ghetto*, trans. Shirley Young (Fitzroy, Australia: Globe Press, 1983), p. 86.

28. Mark Dvorjetski (Dworzecki), "Adjustment of Detainees to Camp and Ghetto Life," *Yad Vashem Studies* 5 (1963):198.

29. Tzvia Kuretzka File, Genia Silkes Collection, YIVO Archives, New York. Murer

often appeared suddenly at the gate and conducted searches. Thousands of workers experienced nightmares every time he unexpectedly descended upon the gate. An accurate description of this ordeal can be found in Masha Rolnik, *Ani Hayevet le-Saper* (Jerusalem: Ahiever, 1965), p. 67; see also Herman Kruk, *Togbuch fun vilner geto* (New York: YIVO, 1961), pp. 222, 237, 239, 245.

30. David Wdowinski, *And We Are Not Saved* (New York: Philosophical Library, 1963), p. 49; Glas-Weiner, *Children of the Ghetto*, pp. 87–89.

31. Glas-Weiner, *Children of the Ghetto*, p. 89.

32. Emilia Gutman File, Genia Silkes Collection, YIVO Archives, New York.

33. David, *Square of Sky*, p. 79; Ringelblum, *Notes from the Warsaw Ghetto*, p. 208.

34. Stephen N. Miller, "The Playful, the Crazy, and the Nature of Pretense" (Paper delivered at American Anthropological Association Meeting, 1973, p. 26); Ringelblum, *Notes from the Warsaw Ghetto*, p. 174.

35. Emma Gluck-La Guardia, *My Story* (New York: McKay, 1961), p. 161.

36. Geve, *Youth in Chains*, pp. 156–57.

37. Contrary to earlier reports, it seems evident that in addition to one in the Czech Family Camp, there were several (perhaps temporary) children's blocks in Auschwitz/Birkenau as well. They were especially evident in the later part of 1944 (interview with Paula Lebovics); report made by Hanna Hofmann-Fischel in Yad Vashem, Jerusalem, quoted also in Schwarberg, *Murders at Bullenhuser Dam*, p. ix.

38. Quoted by Langer, *Versions of Survival*, p. ix.

5 : Play and the Human Spirit

1. Silkes quoted in Friedman, *Amcha*, p. 137.

2. Virulent arguments about what constitutes resistance have raged within historical circles since the conclusion of the war. These were conducted on a philosophical level by historians of various political leanings. None of them really recognized that defiance, protest, and resistance are basically psychological concepts.

3. Kaplan, *Warsaw Diary*, pp. 234–35. There were instances when a theatrical performance, for example, evolved into a spontaneous demonstration (Dawidowicz, *Holocaust Reader*, p. 194).

4. Education constitutes one of the unexplored epics of the Holocaust. In Warsaw regular high school diplomas were distributed in spite of the total ban on secondary education. Jacobson, *Terezin*, p. 14; correspondence with Thomas H. Mandl, Theresienstadt survivor, January 3, 1986.

5. Nakhman Korn, "Dertsiyungsproblemen un kinder-elnt in geto," in *Das Bukh Fun Lublin*, pp. 503–6; quoted in Milton Meltzer, *Never to Forget: The Jews of the Holocaust* (New York: Harper and Row, 1976), p. 99.

6. Kaplan, *Warsaw Diary*, pp. 244–45.

7. Ibid., pp. 153–54.

8. Glas-Weiner, *Children of the Ghetto*, p. 170.

9. Mechanicus, *Year of Fear*, p. 135.

10. "Interview of a child survivor of the Holocaust," conducted by Milton Kestenberg, Jerome Riker International Study of Organized Persecution of Children, New York, letter of February 24, 1986; Glas-Weiner, *Children of the Ghetto*, p. 89.

11. Dr. Aaron Peretz's testimony in the Eichmann trial, quoted by Jacob Robinson, *And the Crooked Shall be Made Straight* (New York: Macmillan, 1965), pp. 122–23; Emilia Gutman File, Genia Silkes Collection, YIVO Archives, New York.
12. Manek Appelbaum File, Genia Silkes Collection, YIVO Archives, New York.
13. Flora Hogman, "Displaced Jewish Children During World War II: How They Coped," *Journal of Humanistic Psychology* 23 (Winter 1983):56–57.
14. Robert Lifton and Eric Olson, *Living and Dying* (New York: Bantam, 1975), pp. 122–23. Lifton defined the concept of "coping" as "psychological numbing." This definition of "coping" was originally applied to adult camp prisoners from Auschwitz. Joel E. Dimsdale argued, however, that "coping" is a much more complex phenomenon. See "The Coping Behavior of Nazi Concentration Camp Survivors," in *Survivors, Victims, and Perpetrators,* ed. Dimsdale (New York: Hemisphere, 1980), pp. 163–74.
15. Hanna Hofmann-Fischel Report, p. 16, Yad Vashem Archives, Jerusalem; Janusz Korczak, *Ghetto Diary* (New York: Holocaust Library), pp. 129–30. This scene made a forceful impression on Korczak; he recorded it twice (see also p. 121).
16. Geve, *Youth in Chains,* pp. 122–23. Although the psychological interpretations of adults' responses to the Holocaust occupy a sizable space in Holocaust literature, no comparable material exists on children. For example, the otherwise in depth work of Dimsdale, *Survivors, Victims, and Perpetrators,* omits any references to child survivors of the Holocaust.
17. Christina Shigar File, Genia Silkes Collection, YIVO Archives, New York.
18. Quoted in Eisenberg, *Witness to the Holocaust,* p. 345.
19. Kaplan, *Warsaw Diary,* p. 352.
20. Ringelblum, *Notes from the Warsaw Ghetto,* pp. 202, 208.
21. Kaplan, *Warsaw Diary,* pp. 182, 294; Kalmanowitch, "Diary of the Nazi Ghetto in Vilna," pp. 23, 42.
22. Ferdeber-Salz, *And the Sun Kept Shining,* p. 96; Adler, *Theresienstadt,* p. 154; Shoshnowski, *Tragedy of Children under Nazi Rule,* pp. 102–4.
23. *Terezin,* pp. 104, 107.
24. Tzvia Kuretzka File, Genia Silkes Collection, YIVO Archives, New York.
25. Katz, *One Who Came Back,* pp. 113–14.
26. Barry Spanjaard, *Don't Fence Me In!* (Saugus, Calif.: B & B, 1981), pp. 131–32.
27. Correspondence with Dr. Gertrude Schneider, April 29, 1986.
28. Jerome Riker International Study of Organized Persecution of Children, File BB-D/AA, p. 43; J. M. Robert and Brian Sutton-Smith, "Game Training and Game Involvement," *Ethnology* 1 (1962):116–85; see Gump and Sutton-Smith, "Activity-Setting and Social Interaction," pp. 755–60; Levy, *Play Behavior,* pp. 124–35.

6 : They Play before They Die

1. Eugene Heimler, "Children of Auschwitz" in *Prison,* ed. George Mikes (London: Routledge and Kegan Paul, 1963), p. 12.
2. See R. E. Herron and Brian Sutton-Smith, *Child's Play* (New York: John Wiley and Sons, 1971); M. J. Ellis, *Why People Play* (Englewood Cliffs, N.J.: Prentice-Hall, 1973).

Scholarly literature on the psychological and anthropological study of play is extensive and rapidly growing.

3. Berg, *Warsaw Ghetto Diary*, p. 147; see Robert Plutchik, *Emotion: A Psychoevolutionary Synthesis* (New York: Harper and Row, 1980), pp. 324–26.

4. Reizel Korczack, *Lehavot be-Efer* (Tel Aviv: Sifriyat Hapoalim, 1946).

5. Quoted in a manuscript by Genia Silkes, "Der Yiddisher Lehrer in Warschawer Geto," Genia Silkes Collection, YIVO Archives, New York.

6. David, *Square of Sky*, p. 186.

7. Mechanicus, *Year of Fear*, p. 87. Similar impressions were conveyed by Saul Friedlaender from a French orphanage for Jewish children, *When Memory Comes*, trans. Helen L. Lane (New York: Farrar Straus and Giroux, 1979), pp. 72–73.

8. Katz, *One Who Came Back*, p. 133; Schneider, *Journey into Terror*, pp. 96–97.

9. Mechanicus, *Year of Fear*, p. 82; David, *Square of Sky*, p. 202.

10. Lutek Stauber File, Genia Silkes Collection, YIVO Archives, New York.

11. Stanislaw Adler, *In the Warsaw Ghetto, 1940–1943*, trans. Sara Philip (Jerusalem: Yad Vashem, 1982), p. 260. In the vernacular of the ghetto, "coalminers" were children who dug for the little pieces of coal and other burnable material that were used for heating and cooking. Trunk, *Lodzher Geto*, p. 344.

12. Dworzecki, *Yerushalayim D'Lita*, p. 329; interview with Gabriele Silten, February 17, 1986.

13. Mechanicus, *Year of Fear*, p. 166; interview with Gabriele Silten.

14. David, *Square of Sky*, p. 136. See L. Garfunkel, *Kovno ha-Yehudit Behurbanah* (Jerusalem: Yad Vashem, 1959), p. 249.

15. Tadeusz Borowski, *This Way for the Gas, Ladies and Gentlemen*, trans. Barbara Vedder (New York: Penguin Books, 1976, p. 86. One should note that Auschwitz proper was inhabited almost entirely by non-Jewish prisoners. From there Jews were directed to Birkenau where they were either placed into slave labor companies or dispatched to the gas chambers. Thus these games were played and attended solely by non-Jewish prisoners. See also Avraham Kohavi, "Na'ar ha-Mahanot," *Yalkut Moreshet* 2 (July 1965): 11–12.

16. Goldstein, *Stars Bear Witness*, p. 82; Glas-Wiener, *Children of the Ghetto*, p. 208.

17. Jan Karski, *The Story of a Secret State*, quoted by Eisenberg, *Witness to the Holocaust*, pp. 169–70.

18. Peretz quoted in Robinson, *And the Crooked Shall Be Made Straight*, pp. 122–23.

19. Kaplan, *Warsaw Diary*, pp. 290–91.

20. Bruno Bettelheim, *Surviving and Other Essays* (New York: Alfred Knopf, 1979), p. 63; Schneider, *Journey into Terror*, pp. 118–19; see also Boas, *Boulevard des Misères*, pp. 72–73.

21. Veronica M. Axline, *Play Therapy* (Boston: Houghton Mifflin, 1947), p. 16.

22. It is neither the purpose nor the rationale of this book to refute or endorse the irrelevance or appropriateness of certain play theories. For an overview of different play theories see Cheska, *Play as Context*; Levy, *Play Behavior*.

23. Karl Groos, *The Play of Man* (New York: Appleton, 1908).

24. See D. W. Fiske and S. R. Maddi, eds., *Functions of Varied Experience* (Homewood, Ill.: Dorsey Press, 1961).

25. Endre Grastyán, *A Játék Neurobiológiája* (Budapest: Akadémiai Könyvkiadó, 1985).
26. P. K. Smith, "Does Play Matter? Functional and Evolutionary Aspects of Animal and Human Play," *Behavioral and Brain Sciences* 5 (1982): 139–84; see also George Eisen et al., *Understanding Leisure: An Interdisciplinary Approach* (Dubuque, Iowa: Kendall/Hunt, 1988).
27. Jerome Riker International Study of Organized Persecution of Children, File BB-D/AA, p. 45; letter from Judith S. Kestenberg, June 11, 1986.
28. Richard S. Lazarus. "Emotions and Adaptation: Conceptual and Empirical Relations," in *Nebraska Symposium on Motivation*, ed. W. J. Arnold (Lincoln: University of Nebraska Press, 1968).
29. J. H. Flawell, *The Developmental Psychology of Jean Piaget* (Princeton: Van Nostrand-Reinhold, 1963), pp. 49–50.
30. Interview with Gabriele Silten.
31. Written by Hanus Hachenburg in Theresienstadt; quoted in *Children's Drawings from the Concentration Camp of Terezin*.
32. Glas-Wiener, *Children of the Ghetto*, p. 90.

7 : Epilogue

1. Olga Lengyel, *Five Chimneys: The Story of Auschwitz* (New York: Howard Fertig, 1983), pp. 111–12. Almost identical dialogue was recorded by Otto Wolken, "What I Think of Children . . . ," in *Auschwitz, An Anthology*, 4:15.
2. Renée Fodor, "The Impact of the Nazi Occupation of Poland on the Jewish Mother-Child Relationship," *YIVO Annual of Jewish Social Sciences* 11 (1956/57): 270–85.
3. Christina Shigar File, Genia Silkes Collection, YIVO Archives, New York; interview with Daisy Miller, April 10, 1986.
4. J. Sarnecki, "Emotional Conflicts of People Born in Nazi Concentration Camps or Imprisoned There During Early Childhood," p. 187; W. Poltawska et al., "Results of Psychiatric Examination of People Born in Nazi Concentration Camps," in *Auschwitz, An Anthology*, 4:60, 187.
5. Interview with Fern Loty, April 17, 1986; Jerome Riker International Study of Organized Persecution of Children, File BB-D/AA, 1/16/85, p. 36; see also Eisen, *Understanding Leisure*, pp. 61–89.
6. See Perry Black, ed. *Physiological Correlates of Emotion* (New York: Academic Press, 1970); Heimler, "Children of Auschwitz," in Mikes, *Prison*, p. 12.
7. Lengyel, *Five Chimneys*, p. 209.

Bibliography

1. Primary Sources

A. Interviews and Correspondence

Beim-Langer, Adele. Letter of June 16, 1986.
Kestenberg, Judith S. Letters of February 24, and June 11, 1986.
Lebovics, Paula. Interview on January 20, 1988.
Loty, Fern. Interview on April 17, 1986.
Mandl, Thomas. Letter of January 3, 1986.
Milich, Esther. Interviews on November 7, and December 15, 1985.
Miller, Daisy. Interview on April 10, 1986.
Schneider, Gertrude. Letter of April 29, 1986.
Silten, Gabriele R. Interview on February 17, 1986.
Trepman, Paul. Letter of January 6, 1986.

B. Archives Consulted

American Friends Service Committee Archives, Philadelphia.
Archive Central Jewish Historical Commission, Warsaw: Children's Testimonies.
Beth Lohamei Hagetaot (Ghetto Fighters' Museum), Israel: Photographic Collection.
Bildarchiv Preussische Kulturbesitz, West Germany.
Jerome Riker Foundation, International Study of Organized Persecution of Children, New York.
Leo Baeck Institute, New York: Eva Noack-Mosse, "Theresienstaedter Tagebuch"; Konzentrationslager Camp des Mills File; Philantropin Collection.
Musée d'Histoire Contemporaine, Paris.

"Precious Legacy Project," B'nai B'rith Klutznik Museum, Washington, D.C.
Rijksintituut voor Oorlogsdocumentatie, Amsterdam: Photographic Collection.
The Simon Wiesenthal Center, Los Angeles: "Situation of Polish Children and Nazi Crimes Committed on Polish Children During World War Two," in International Scientific Symposium, 1979 File.
Yad Vashem, Jerusalem: Hanna Hofmann-Fischel Report; Photographic Archives.
YIVO Archives, New York: The Lodz Collection; The Genia Silkes Collection.

2. Books

Abbels, Byers Chana. *The Children We Remember*. Rockville, Md.: Kar-Ben, 1983.
Adler, H. G. *Theresienstadt, 1941–1945*. Tuebingen: J.C.B. Mohr, 1955.
Adler, Stanislaw. *In the Warsaw Ghetto, 1940–1943*. Translated by Sara Philip, Jerusalem: Yad Vashem, 1982.
Arad, Yitzhak, *Ghetto in Flames*. New York: Holocaust Library, 1982.
Auerbach, Rachel. *Be'hutzot Warsaw*. Tel Aviv: Am Oved, 1946.
Auschwitz, An Anthology on Inhuman Medicine. 4 vols. Warsaw: International Auschwitz Committee, 1971.
Axline, Veronica M. *Play Therapy*. Boston: Houghton Mifflin, 1947.
Bauer, Yehuda. *The Jewish Emergence from Powerlessness*. Toronto: University of Toronto Press, 1979.
Bauminger, Aryeh, Nachman Blumenthal, and Josef Karmish. *Ha-Yeled ve-Hano'ar be-Shoah ve-ha-Gevurah*. Jerusalem: Kiryat Sefer, 1965.
Belsen. Tel Aviv: Irgun Sheerit Hapleita, 1957.
Berg, Mary. *Warsaw Ghetto Diary*. Edited by S. L. Shneiderman. New York: L. B. Fischer, 1945.
Bettelheim, Bruno. *Surviving and Other Essays*. New York: Alfred A. Knopf, 1979.
Blatter, Janet, and Sybil Milton, eds. *Art of the Holocaust*. New York: Rutledge, 1981.
Blumenthal, Nachman. *Darko Shel Yudnrat*. Jerusalem: Yad Vashem, 1962.
Boas, Jacob. *Boulevard des Misères: The Story of Transit Camp Westerbork*. New York: Archon Books, 1985.
Boehm, Eric H. *We Survived: The Stories of the Hidden and the Hunted of Nazi Germany*. Santa Barbara, Calif.: Clio Press, 1966.
Borowski, Tadeusz. *This Way for the Gas Ladies and Gentlemen*. Translated by Barbara Vedder. New York: Penguin Books, 1976.
Braun, Zvi, and Dov Levin. *Toldoteha shel Mahteret*. Jerusalem: Yad Vashem, 1962.
Brietowitz, Jacob. *Through Hell to Life*. New York: Shengold, 1983.
Brenner, L. *Widershtand un umkum fun Czenstokhover Geto*. Warsaw: 1951.
Bruner, Jerome S., et al. *Play: Its Role in Development and Evolution*. New York: Basic Books, 1976.
Cheska, Alyce Taylor, ed. *Play as Context*. West Point, N.Y.: Leisure Press, 1981.
Children's Drawings from the Concentration Camp of Terezin. Prague: State Jewish Museum, n.d.

Cohen, Elie A. *Human Behavior in the Concentration Camp*. New York: Norton, 1953.
Constanza, Mary S. *The Living Witness: Art in the Concentration Camps and Ghettos*. New York: Free Press, 1982.
Czerniakow, Adam. *The Warsaw Diary of Adam Czerniakow*. Edited by Raul Hilberg, Stanislaw Staron, and Josef Kermisz. New York: Stein and Day, 1979.
David, Janina. *A Square of Sky*. New York: Norton, 1964.
Dawidowicz, Lucy S. *The Holocaust and the Historians*. Cambridge: Harvard University Press, 1981.
———. *The War Against the Jews, 1933–1945*. New York: Holt, Rinehart and Winston, 1975.
———, ed. *A Holocaust Reader*. New York: Behrman House, 1976.
Dimsdale, Joel E., ed. *Survivors, Victims, and Perpetrators*. New York: Hemisphere, 1980.
Dobroszycki, Lucjan, ed. *The Chronicle of the Lodz Ghetto, 1941–1944*. New Haven: Yale University Press, 1984.
Donat, Alexander. *The Holocaust Kingdom: A Memoir*. New York: Holocaust Library, 1978.
Dworzecki, Mark. *Europa Lelo Yeladim*. Jerusalem: Yad Vashem, 1958.
———. *Mahanot ha-Yehudim be-Estonia, 1942–1944*. Jerusalem: Yad Vashem, 1970.
———. *Yerushalayim D'Lita be-Meri va-Shoah*. Tal Aviv: Mifleget Poalei Eretz-Yisrael, 1951.
Eck, Nathan. *Ha-To'im be-Darkei ha-Mavet*. Jerusalem: Yad Vashem, 1960.
Edelbaum, Ben. *Growing Up in the Holocaust*. Kansas City: Ben Edelman, 1980.
Eisen, George, et al. *Understanding Leisure: An Interdisciplinary Approach*. Dubuque, Iowa: Kendall/Hunt, 1988.
Eisenberg, Azriel, ed. *Witness to the Holocaust*. New York: Pilgrim Press, 1981.
Ellis, James M. *Why People Play*. Englewood Cliffs, N.J.: Prentice-Hall, 1973.
Erickson, E. H. *Childhood and Society*. New York: Norton, 1950.
Erlichman-Bank, Sarah. *Bi-Yedei Teme'im*. Tel Aviv: Hakibbutz Hameuchad, 1976.
Faschismus—Getto—Massenmord: Dokumentation ueber Ausrottung und Widerstand der Juden in Polen waehrend des 2. Weltkrieges. Edited by Zydowski Instytut Historyczny Warsaw. Frankfurt/Main, 1962.
Feig, Konnylyn G. *Hitler's Death Camps: The Sanity of Madness*. New York: Holmes and Meier, 1979.
Ferderber-Salz, Bertha. *And the Sun Kept Shining. . . .* New York: Holocaust Library, 1980.
Fiske, D. W., and S. R. Maddi, eds. *Functions of Varied Experience*. Homewood, Ill.: Dorsey Press, 1961.
Flawell, J. H. *The Developmental Psychology of Jean Piaget*. Princeton: Van Nostrand-Reinhold, 1963.
Flinker, Moses. *Ha-Na'ar Moshe*. Jerusalem: Yad Vashem, 1958.
Frank, Anne. *The Diary of a Young Girl*. Translated by B. M. Manyaart. Garden City, N.Y.: Doubleday, 1967.
Frankl, Victor E. *Man's Search for Meaning*. Translated by Ilse Lasch. New York: Simon and Schuster, 1963.

Friedlaender, Saul. *When Memory Comes*. Translated by Helen R. Lane. New York: Farrar, Straus, and Giroux, 1979.

Friedman, Ina R. *Escape or Die: True Stories of Young People Who Survived the Holocaust*. Reading, Mass.: Addison-Wesley, 1982.

Friedman, Saul S. *Amcha: An Oral Testament of the Holocaust*. Washington, D.C.: University Press of America, 1979.

Fromm, Bella. *Blood and Banquets: A Berlin Social Diary*. New York: Harper and Row, 1942.

Garfunkel, L. *Kovno ha-Yehudit be-Hurbanah*. Jerusalem: Yad Vashem, 1959.

Geve, Thomas. *Youth in Chains*. Jerusalem: Rubin Mass, 1981.

Gilbert, G. M. *Nuremberg Diary*. New York: Signet Books, 1961.

Glas-Wiener, Sheva. *Children of the Ghetto*. Translated by the author and Shirley Young. Fitzroy, Australia: Globe Press, 1983.

Glatstein, Jacob, et al., ed. *Anthology of Holocaust Literature*. New York: Atheneum, 1975.

Gluck-La Guardia, Emma, *My Story*, New York: McKay, 1961.

Goldstein, Bernard. *The Stars Bear Witness*, New York: Viking Press, 1949.

Grastyán, Endre. *A Játék Neurobiológiája*. Budapest: Akadémiai Könyvkiadó, 1985.

Green, Gerald. *The Artists of Terezin*. New York: Hawthorn Books, 1969.

Groos, R. *The Play of Man*. New York: Appleton, 1908.

Grossman, Mendel. *With a Camera in the Ghetto*. Tel Aviv: Hakibbutz Hameuchad, 1970.

Gutman, Israel. *The Jews of Warsaw, 1939–1943*. Translated by Ina Friedman. Bloomington: Indiana University Press, 1982.

———. "Youth Movements in the Underground and the Ghetto Revolts." In *Jewish Resistance during the Holocaust*. Jerusalem: Yad Vashem, 1971.

Gutman, Israel, and Livia Rothkirchen, eds. *Sho'at Yehude Europa*. Jerusalem: Yad Vashem, 1973/74.

Halperin, Irving. *Messengers from the Death*. Philadelphia: Westminster Press, 1970.

Hart, Kitty. *I Am Alive*. Bakerville, Gt. Britain: Corgi Books, 1961.

———. *Return to Auschwitz*. New York: Atheneum, 1982.

Hausner, Gideon. *Justice in Jerusalem*. New York: Harper and Row, 1966.

Herron, R. E., and Brian Sutton-Smith. *Child's Play*. New York: John Wiley and Sons, 1971.

Hillesum, Etty. *An Interrupted Life: The Diaries of Etty Hillesum*. Translated by Arno Pomerans. New York: Pantheon Books, 1983.

Hoess, Rudolf. *Commandant of Auschwitz*. Translated by Constantin Fitz-Gibbon. Cleveland: World, 1959.

Hrabar, Roman, Zofia Tokarz, and Jacek E. Wilczur. *The Fate of Polish Children During the Last War*. Warsaw: Interpress, 1981.

Huizinga, Johan. *Homo Ludens: A Study of the Play Element in Culture*. New York: Routledge and Kegan Paul, 1949.

Jacobson, Jacob. *Terezin: The Daily Life, 1943–1945*. London: Jewish Central Information Office, 1946.

Kantor, Alfred. *The Book of Alfred Kantor*. New York: McGraw-Hill, 1971.

Kaplan, Chaim A. *The Warsaw Diary of Chaim Kaplan*. Edited and translated by Abraham I. Katsh. New York: Collier Books, 1973.

Karski, Jan. *Story of a Secret State*. Boston: Houghton Mifflin, 1944.

Katz, Alfred. *Poland's Ghettos at War*. New York: Twayne Press, 1970.

Katz, Josef. *One Who Came Back: The Diary of a Jewish Survivor*. New York: Herzl Press and Bergen-Belsen Memorial Press, 1973.

Kelemen, Gábor L. *Gól A Halál Kapujában*. Budapest: Egyetemi Nyomda, 1981.

Keller, Ulrich, ed. *The Warsaw Ghetto in Photographs*. New York: Dover, 1984.

Keneally, Thomas. *Schindler's List*. New York: Penguin Books, 1983.

Kinder im KZ. West Berlin: Elefanten Press, 1979.

Klarsfeld, Serge, ed. *Les enfants d'Izieu une tragédie juive*. The Beate Klarsfeld Foundation, 1983.

Klein-Weissman, Gerda. *All But My Life*. New York: Hill and Wang, 1957.

Klinger, Chaika. *Me-Yoman be-Geto*. Tel Aviv: Sifriyat Hapoalim, 1959.

Korczak, Janusz. *Ghetto Diary*. Translated by Jerzy Bachrach and Barbara Krzywicka. New York: Holocaust Library, 1978.

Korczak, Reizel. *Lehavot be-Efer*. Tel Aviv: Sifriyat Hapoalim, 1946.

Kotlar, Helen. *We Lived in a Grave*. Translated by Dr. Judah Pilch. New York: Shengold, 1980.

Kowalski, Isaac. *A Secret Press in Nazi Europe*. New York: Central Guide, 1969.

Kraus, Ota, and Erik Kulka. *Bet Haroshet le-Mavet: Auschwitz*. Jerusalem: Yad Vashem, 1960/61.

Kren, George M., and Leon Rappaport. *The Holocaust and the Crisis of Human Endeavor*. New York: Holmes and Meier, 1980.

Kruk, Herman. *Togbukh fun Vilna Geto*. New York: YIVO, 1961.

Kuckler-Silberman, Lena. *One Hundred Children*. Garden City, N.Y.: Doubleday, 1961.

Kuznetsov, Anatoli. *Babi Yar*. Translated by David Floyd. New York: Farrar, Straus and Giroux, 1970.

Langbeim, Hermann. *Menschen in Auschwitz*. Wein: Europaverlag, 1972.

Langer, Lawrence L. *Versions of Survival: The Holocaust and the Human Spirit*. Albany: State University of New York Press, 1982.

Latour, Anny. *The Jewish Resistance in France (1940–1944)*. Translated by Irene R. Ilton. New York: Holocaust Library, 1981.

Lazarson-Rostovsky, Tamar. *Yomana Shel Tamara*. Tel Aviv: Kibbutz Hameuchad, 1976.

Lazarus, Richard S. "Emotions and Adaptation: Conceptual and Empirical Relations." *Nebraska Symposium on Motivation*. Edited by W. J. Arnold. Lincoln: University of Nebraska Press, 1968.

Lengyel, Olga. *Five Chimneys*. New York: Howard Fertig, 1983.

Leonard, Wilbert M. A Sociological Perspective of Sport. Second ed. Minneapolis: Burgess, 1984.

Levai, Eugene. *Black Book on the Martyrdom of Hungarian Jewry*. Zurich: Central European Times, 1948.

———. *Zsidósors Európában*. Budapest: Magyar Téka, 1948.

Levin, Abraham. *Me-Pinkaso shel ha-More me-Yehudiyah.* Tel Aviv: Hakibbutz Hameuchad, 1969.
Levin, Nora. *The Holocaust.* New York: Thomas Y. Corwell, 1968.
Levy, Joseph. *Play Behavior.* New York: John Wiley and Sons, 1978.
Levy-Haas, Hanna. *Inside Belsen.* Totowa, N.J.: Barnes and Noble, 1982.
Leyzer, Ran. *Jerusalem of Lithuania.* 2 vols. New York: Laurate Press, 1974.
Lifton, Robert J., and Eric Olson. *Living and Dying.* New York: Bantam Books, 1975.
Mazia, Fredka. *Re'im ba-Sa'ar.* Jerusalem: Yad Vashem, 1964.
McGhee, P. E. *Humor: Its Origin and Development.* San Francisco: W. H. Freeman, 1979.
Mechanicus, Philip. *Year of Fear: A Jewish Prisoner Waits for Auschwitz.* Translated by Irene S. Gibbons. New York: Hawthorn, 1968.
Meed, Vladka [Feigele Peltel Myendzizshetski]. *On Both Sides of the Wall.* Translated by Steven Meed. New York: Holocaust Library, 1979.
Meier, Lili, and Peter Hellman. *The Auschwitz Album.* New York: Random House, 1981.
Meltzer, Milton. *Never to Forget: The Jews of the Holocaust.* New York: Harper and Row, 1976.
Mikes, George, ed. *Prison.* London: Routledge and Kegan Paul, 1963.
Moskovitz, Sara. *Love Despite Hate.* New York: Schocken Books, 1983.
Mueller, Filip. *Eyewitness in Auschwitz: Three Years in the Gas Chambers.* Translated by Susanne Flatauer. New York: Stein and Day, 1979.
Neshamit, Sarah. *Ma'avako shel ha-Geto.* Lochamei Hagetaot: Hakibbutz Hameuchad, 1972.
Nomberg-Przytyk, Sara. *Auschwitz: True Tales from a Grotesque Land.* Translated by Roslyn Hirsch. Chapel Hill: University of North Carolina Press, 1985.
Piaget, Jean. *Play, Dreams, and Imitation in Childhood.* New York: Norton, 1962.
Plutchik, Robert. *Emotion: A Psychoevolutionary Synthesis.* New York: Harper and Row, 1980.
Presser, Jacob. *The Destruction of the Dutch Jews.* Translated by Arnold Pomerans. New York: E. P. Dutton, 1969.
Ringelblum, Emmanuel. *Notes from the Warsaw Ghetto.* Edited by Jacob Sloan. New York: Schocken Books, 1974.
Robinson, Jacob. *And the Crooked Shall Be Made Straight.* New York: Macmillan, 1965.
Rolnik, Masha. *Ani Hayevet Lesaper.* Jerusalem: Achiever, 1965.
Rosenblatt, Roger. *Children of War.* New York: Doubleday, 1983.
Rosenbluth, Martin. *Go Forth and Serve: Early Years and Public Life.* New York: Herzl Press, 1961.
Rothchild, Sylvia, ed. *Voices from the Holocaust.* New York: New American Library, 1981.
Rubinowitz, David. *The Diary of David Rubinowitz.* Translated by Derek Bowman. Edmonds, Wash.: Creative Options, 1982.
Rubinstein, Erna F. *The Survivor in Us All.* New York: Archon Books, 1983.
Rudashevski, Yitshok. *The Diary of the Vilna Ghetto.* Translated by Perry Matenko. Tel Aviv: Shamgar Press, 1973.

Schiller, Friedrich J. C. *Letters Upon the Aesthetic Education of Man*. Harvard Classics Series, vol. 32. New York: P. F. Collier, 1910.

Schneider, Gertrude. *Journey into Terror: The Story of the Riga Ghetto*. New York: Ark House, 1979.

Schoenberner, Gerhard. *The Yellow Star: The Persecution of the Jews in Europe, 1933–1945*. Translated by Susan Sweet. New York: Bantam Books, 1979.

Schwarberg, Guenther. *The Murders at Bullenhuser Dam*. Translated by Erna Baber Rosenfeld and Alvin H. Rosenfeld. Bloomington: Indiana University Press, 1984.

Seidman, Hillel. *Yoman Ghetto Warsaw*. New York: Die Yiddishe Woche, 1957.

Shoshnowski, Kiryl. *The Tragedy of Children under Nazi Rule*. Poznan: Zachodnia, 1962.

Sós, Endre. *Európai Fasizmus és Antiszemitizmus*. Budapest: Magyar Téka, n.d.

Spanjaard, Barry. *Don't Fence Me In*. Saugus, Calif.: B & B, 1981.

Suhl, Yuri, ed. *They Fought Back*. New York: Crown, 1967.

Syrkin, Marie. *Blessed Is the Match: The Story of Jewish Resistance*. New York: Alfred A. Knopf, 1947.

Székely, Éva. *Sirni Csak a Gyöztesnek Szabad*. Budapest: Magvetö, 1982.

Terezin. Prague: Council of Jewish Communities in the Czech Lands, 1965.

Terezin, 1941–1945. Prague: The State Jewish Museum, 1983.

Toll, Nelly. *Without Surrender: Art of the Holocaust*. Philadelphia: Running Press, 1978.

Trepman, Paul. *Among Men and Beasts*. Translated by Shoshana Perla and Gertrude Hirschler. New York: A. S. Barnes, 1978.

Trunk, Isaiah. *Jewish Responses to Nazi Persecution*. New York: Stein and Day, 1979.

———. *Judenrat: The Jewish Councils in Eastern Europe under the Nazi Occupation*. New York: Macmillan, 1972.

———. *Lodzher Geto*. New York: YIVO Archives, 1962.

Turkow, Jonas. *Haya Hayta Warsaw Yehudit*. Tel Aviv: Tarbut Vehihuch, 1969.

Tushnet, Leonard. *The Pavement of Hell*. New York: St. Martin's Press, 1972.

Vegh, Claudine. *I Didn't Say Goodbye*. New York: E. P. Dutton, 1979.

Volavkova, H., ed. *I Never Saw Another Butterfly: Children's Drawings and Poems from Terezin Concentration Camp, 1942–1944*. New York: McGraw-Hill, 1964.

Vrba, Rudolf, and Alan Bestic. *I Cannot Forgive*. New York: Grove Press, 1964.

Wdowinski, David. *And We Are Not Saved*. New York: Philosophical Library, 1963.

Weinstein, Frida Scheps. *A Hidden Childhood, 1942–1945*. Translated by Barbara Loeb Kennedy. New York: Hill and Wang, 1985.

Weissberg, Alex. *Advocate for the Dead*. London: André Deutsch, 1958.

Wells, Weliczker Leon. *The Janowska Road*. New York: Macmillan, 1963.

Yerusalmi, Eliezer. *Pinkas Shavli*. Jerusalem: Yad Vashem, 1958.

Zuckerman, Yitzhak, and Moshe Basok, eds. *Sefer Milchamot Hagetaot*. Tel Aviv: Hakibbutz Hameuchad, 1954.

Zylberberg, M. *A Warsaw Diary, 1939–1945*. London: Hartmore, 1969.

Zyskind, Sara. *Stolen Years*. Minneapolis: Lerner, 1981.

3. Periodicals and Proceedings

Ash, Saul. "The Dignity of the Destroyed: Towards a Definition of the Period of the Holocaust." *Judaism* 2 (1962): 166–75.

Bachner, Eli. "Be-Theresienstadt, be-Mahane ha-Mishpachiti be-Auschwitz, bein ha-Sonderkommando, be-Buchenwald." *Yalkut Moreshet* 22 (November 1976): 75–96.

Beinfeld, Solon. "The Cultural Life of the Vilna Ghetto." *Simon Wiesenthal Center Annual* 1 (1983):5–26.

Bialer, Tosha. "Behind the Wall." *Collier's*, February 20, and February 27, 1943.

Bloom, Solomon F. "Dictator of the Lodz Ghetto." *Commentary* 7 (February 1949): 111–22.

Dvorjetski (Dworzecki), Mark. "Adjustment of Detainees to Camp and Ghetto Life." *Yad Vashem Studies* 5 (1963):193–220.

Fodor, Renée. "The Impact of the Nazi Occupation of Poland on the Jewish Mother-Child Relationship." *YIVO Annual of Jewish Social Sciences* 2 (1956/57):270–85.

Friedman, Philip. "Two 'Saviors' Who Failed." *Commentary* 26 (May 1958):479–91.

Gump, P. V., and Brian Sutton-Smith. "Activity-Setting and Social Interaction." *American Journal of Orthopsychiatry* 25 (1955):755–60.

Hershkovitch, Bendet. "The Ghetto in Litzmannstadt (Lodz)." *YIVO Annual of Jewish Social Sciences* 4 (1950):85–122.

Hogman, Flora. "Displaced Jewish Children During World War II: How They Coped." *Journal of Humanistic Psychology* 23 (Winter 1983):51–66.

Kalmanowitch, Zelig. "A Diary of the Nazi Ghetto in Vilna." *YIVO Annual of Jewish Social Sciences* 8 (1953):9–81.

Kohavi, Avraham. "Na'ar ha-Mahanot." *Yalkut Moreshet* 2 (July 1965):7–20.

Krell, Robert. "Therapeutic Value of Documenting Child Survivors." *Journal of the American Academy of Child Psychiatry* 24 (July 1985):397–405.

"Letters from Jewish Children May Return to Haunt 'Butcher of Lyon.' " *Los Angeles Times*, January 20, 1985.

Mayer Yogi, Paul. "Equality-Egality: Jews and Sport in Germany." *Leo Baeck Institute Year Book* 25 (1980):221–41.

Miller, Stephen N. "The Playful, the Crazy, and the Nature of Pretense." Paper delivered at American Anthropological Association Meeting, 1973.

Moskovicz, Sarah. "Longitudinal Follow-up of Child Survivors of the Holocaust." *Journal of the American Academy of Child Psychiatry* 24 (July 1985):401–7.

Neuberger, Hirsch. "Be-geto Kovno." *Yalkut Moreshet* 18 (November 1978):149–62.

Neuman-Weiss, Leah. "Al Nashim Yehudiot be-Mahanot Germania." *Yalkut Moreshet* 4 (December 1966):47–69.

Poliakov, L. "The Mind of the Mass Murderer." *Commentary* 12 (November 1951): 451–59.

Pudah, Feivel. "Hirhurim al Yehuda shel ha-Mahteret be-Geto Lodz." *Yalkut Moreshet* 11 (November 1969):59–67.

———. "Kan ha-Shomer ha-Tza'ir be-Geto Lodz." *Yalkut Moreshet* 28 (November 1979):7–39.

Rothkirchen, Livia. "Escape Routes and Contacts During the War." In *Jewish Resistance During the Holocaust,* Proceedings of the Conference on Manifestations of Jewish Resistance. Jerusalem, 1968.

Samuels, Gertrude. "Children Who Have Known No Childhood." *New York Times Magazine,* March 9, 1947.

Sells, S. B. "An Interactionist Looks at the Environment." *American Psychologist* 18 (1963):696–702.

Smith, Peter K. "Does Play Matter? Functional and Evolutionary Aspects of Animal and Human Play." *Behavioral and Brain Sciences* 5 (1982):139–84.

Shtenkler, Ephraim. "What Happened to Me in My Childhood." *Commentary* 9 (May 1952):442–46.

Szwambaum, Halina. "Four Letters from the Warsaw Ghetto." *Commentary* 31 (June 1961):486–92.

Trunk, Isaiah. "Epidemics and Mortality in the Warsaw Ghetto 1939–1942." *YIVO Annual of Jewish Social Sciences* 8 (1953):82–122.

———. "Religious, Educational and Cultural Problems in the Eastern European Ghettos under German Occupation." *YIVO Annual of Jewish Social Sciences* 14(1969): 159–95.

Index